MOUN...

■ COLORADO'S HI...
  MINING DISTR...

Biking

Damage noted 4/23/03

LAURA ROSSETTER

FULCRUM PUBLISHING
GOLDEN, COLORADO

Cover photograph by Robert Green
Book design by Karen Groves
Maps by Doug Iler

Library of Congress Cataloging-in-Publication Data

Rossetter, Laura.
　　Mountain biking Colorado's historic mining districts / Laura Rossetter.
　　　　p.　　cm.
　　Includes bibliographical references (p.).
　　ISBN 1-55591-090-4 (pbk.)
　　　　1. All terrain cycling — Colorado — Guide-books. 2. Bicycle touring —
Colorado — Guide-books. 3. Colorado — Description and travel — 1981– —
Guide-books. I. Title.
GV1045.5.C6R67　1991　　　　　　　　　　　　　　90-85222
796.6'09788 — dc20　　　　　　　　　　　　　　　　CIP

Printed in the United States of America

0　9　8　7　6　5　4　3　2　1

Fulcrum Publishing
350 Indiana Street
Golden, Colorado 80401

CONTENTS

ACKNOWLEDGMENTS

A book of this nature is a combination of many people's efforts. Numerous individuals, organizations, and businesses provided information, advice, and support. Without their assistance this book would not have been possible. To all I offer my sincere gratitude and appreciation.

Some of the most critical information was provided by people who critiqued my ride lists and supplemented them with ideas of their own. Many mountain bikers pored over maps and shared their knowledge of local terrain. Forest Service personnel statewide contributed crucial details on bikeable routes and land access. Bike shops throughout Colorado were always willing to lend advice and support. All of you saved me research time and hours of being lost and deserve my special thanks.

Many others also contributed to this book. Willy Lynch planted the original idea. Bill Stoehr of Trails Illustrated generously provided a stack of his wonderful maps. Dave Bucknam and Pat Archer of Mined Land Reclamation supplied helpful contacts and gave critical information on safety around mining sites. Tony Neaves, bike mechanic extraordinaire, kept my bike running and in one piece. Several mining companies gave candid input on land access issues. Skilled librarians in many small libraries allowed me to delve into their impressive western history collections. Many chambers of commerce, city halls, county governments, and tourism offices went out of their way to get the information I needed. All of the folks at Fulcrum Publishing, particularly Karen Groves, spent hours patiently answering my questions. Graphic artist Doug Iler created top-rate maps and hill profiles. Many biking companions willingly became guinea pigs and accompanied me into the great unknown. Strangers I met on the trail shared their knowledge of routes or provided historical anecdotes. I am grateful to you all.

Two people in particular not only helped the book become reality but also made my riding experiences memorable. My father, Bob Green, in addition to taking the cover photo, spent his first month of retirement as my biking and camping companion during a stint in the San Juans; as we pedaled 200 miles together, he convinced me that turning 60 means you can do more, not less. The companionship of my husband, Steve, always made a backcountry ride special. His unending patience and continuous support helped my idea become a finished product.

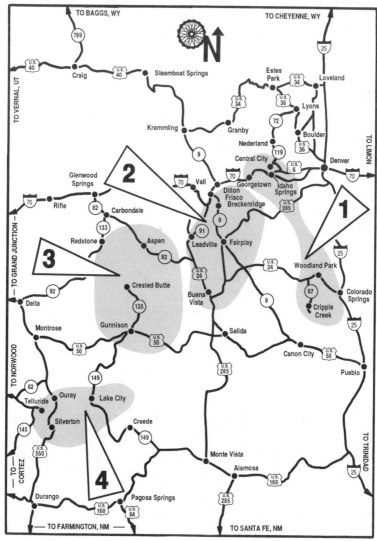

TO BAGGS, WY   TO CHEYENNE, WY

789

TO VERNAL, UT

U.S. 40   Craig   U.S. 40   Steamboat Springs   Estes Park   U.S. 34   Loveland

25

U.S. 34   U.S. 36   Lyons

Kremmling   Granby   72   Boulder

Nederland   119   U.S. 36

9   Central City   U.S. 6   Denver   TO LIMON

Glenwood Springs   **2**   70   Vail   70   Georgetown   Idaho Springs   Denver   70

70   Rifle   82   Carbondale   Dillon Frisco Breckenridge   9   U.S. 285

TO GRAND JUNCTION

133   91

Redstone   **3**   Aspen   Leadville   Fairplay   U.S. 24   Woodland Park   25

82   U.S. 24   Buena Vista   9   67   Colorado Springs

92   Crested Butte   Cripple Creek

Delta   135   25

Montrose   Gunnison   U.S. 50   Salida   Canon City   U.S. 50

U.S. 50   U.S. 50   Pueblo

TO NORWOOD

149   U.S. 285

62   Ouray   Lake City

Telluride   Silverton   Creede

145   149

U.S. 550   **4**   Monte Vista

TO CORTEZ   Alamosa   U.S. 160   25

TO TRINIDAD

Durango   Pagosa Springs   U.S. 285

U.S. 160   U.S. 84

TO FARMINGTON, NM   TO SANTA FE, NM

N

KEY TO ALL AREA, REGION AND RIDE MAPS

Colorado and Region Maps

- **70** U.S. interstate
- **24** U.S. highway
- **9** State or local road
- —— Paved road
- ══ Dirt road
- 🎿 Ski area
- ⌣ Mountain pass
- ▲ Campground
- **24** Ride trailhead

Individual Ride Maps

- ■ Trailhead
- — Described route
- ✗ Prominent historic site
- →→ Recommended route direction

INTRODUCTION

Mountain bikes are fast becoming the method of choice for exploring Colorado's backcountry. Sporting knobby tires and a multitude of gears, yet as comfortable as your childhood one-speed, all-terrain bikes are ideally suited for pedaling the mind-boggling array of backwoods roads and trails crisscrossing Colorado. Every year more fat-tire enthusiasts make the pilgrimage to Colorado's high country to experience the undeniable thrill of crossing a windswept ridge or cruising through a field of wildflowers on a bicycle. Blessed with more backroads and trails than could be pedaled in a lifetime, Colorado has evolved into a prime location for mountain biking.

Long before Colorado became a mountain bike mecca it was crawling with a different breed of explorer. Gold-hungry prospectors flocked to the Rockies to unlock its treasure chest of mineral wealth. These hardy souls, in pursuit of the elusive mother lode, climbed the high peaks and traversed hidden valleys. They established camps, erected mines, and built towns. Trails and roads were constructed to bring supplies in and haul the riches out. Today, countless weathered settlements and rugged mountain pathways remain as evidence of the miners' determination to extract wealth from every nook and cranny of Colorado. This mining legacy has become one of the state's unique assets. Rarely can you explore a peak or valley without seeing an eroded relic clinging to the side of a cliff or decaying in a meadow. Frequently, the route to these sites was constructed a century or more ago. The network of historic byways that laces the Rockies is partially responsible for Colorado's reputation as a mountain bike paradise. Thanks to the efforts of some early high-country adventurers, we now have endless miles of old pack trails, overgrown wagon routes, and deserted railroad grades that provide the ideal means for pedaling Colorado's high country.

Mountain Biking Colorado's Historic Mining Districts is a resource for backcountry bikers interested in pedaling through the past. A working guide to mountain-bike routes around Colorado's mining camps and ghost towns, this book leads you across the state in pursuit of the sometimes elusive remains of a glorious mining era. Isolated cabins, well-preserved ghost towns, and crumbling mine sites mark the way as backroad byways first traveled more than one hundred years ago take you deep into the Colorado Rockies. Route directions combined with historic narratives guide you on a variety of tours that explore the mineral belt stretching from the Front Range to the rugged San Juans. Varied terrain ranging from a gentle cruise along an abandoned railroad grade to a challenging climb up a mountain pass provides options for mountain bikers of all abilities. This guidebook captures the unique ingredients of Colorado, its magnificent high country and intriguing mining heritage, and weaves them into a series of mountain-bike rides that explore the beauty of the Rockies while providing a fascinating glimpse into the past.

Backcountry Bicycling Tips

Rules and Regulations

As the newest on an ever-growing list of backcountry users, mountain bikers are under a lot of scrutiny. Responsibility is the key word in keeping attitudes toward off-road cyclists on a positive level. Mountain bikers venturing into the backcountry should be equipped with the basic knowledge to be responsible for their own actions and safety and for the environment in which they ride.

Summarized below are a few simple but important rules concerning trail etiquette for mountain bikers. Phrased in many different ways but always conveying the same message, these rules now appear on water bottles, are attached to tags on new bikes, and are in every publication relating to mountain bikes. They developed as the result of rapid growth in the sport and the need for a consistent thread of understanding among backcountry bikers. Adherence to these rules is vital to promote responsible backcountry biking.

HIKERS: Yield the right of way to hikers. When approaching hikers from behind, make your presence known well in advance and inform them of your intention to pass.

HORSEBACK RIDERS: Most horses are easily spooked by bicycles. When you encounter riders, leave the trail so they can pass. Pass horses only after telling the riders of your intentions and allowing them to bring their horses under control.

MOUNTAIN BIKERS: When descending, yield to bikers coming up. When overtaking another bike, communicate your intention and choose an area that provides enough space for passing. Yield the trail to bikers wishing to pass you.

VEHICLES: Jeeps, motorbikes, and all-terrain vehicles are common in parts of Colorado's high country and use some of the same routes that are popular with mountain bikers. If you encounter a vehicle allow it plenty of room to pass, especially on a narrow road. You'll find that mountain bikes are often faster than vehicles on downhill sections. When passing, be aware that they usually have no idea you're near.

In addition to awareness of other trail users, it's important to take precautions that help preserve the natural surroundings. Adopt the "soft cycling" approach toward backcountry biking, which means minimizing your impact on the environment. Be sensitive toward your surroundings and keep in mind a few important tips.

1. Stay on designated roads and trails to protect surrounding soil and vegetation. Refrain from riding through mud holes, bogs, etc., which could leave long-lasting ruts. Minimize potential erosion by not shortcutting switchbacks. Avoid riding over vegetation, especially above timberline, where plant life is extremely fragile.

2. Ride in control. Check your speed. Avoid locking your brakes, which causes unnecessary trail damage.

3. Try not to spook stock and wildlife. I see a wild animal almost every time I ride, and stopping a distance away from it gives me an opportunity to observe and the animal a chance for a safe exit. Cows grazing in the high country are a common sight in Colorado. Stop or ride by them slowly so they have time to respond without panicking.

4. Wilderness areas are closed to mountain bikers. The ride descriptions tell you if you're near a wilderness boundary so you can avoid it.

5. Respect private property. Colorado has a lot of it, especially around mining country where most old mines and settlements sit on private land. Some areas, such as Cripple Creek and the Idaho Springs–Central City region, have large concentrations of private land containing mines that often are being reopened and worked. This situation limited my ability to include many of the historical rides in these areas, and you may notice or already know of an interesting trail or road leading to a historical site that is not described in this book. This is usually due to lack of legal public access into these areas. Consequently, these routes should not be pursued. Don't venture off designated roads and trails. Consult a map or ask someone when unsure of land ownership. Some of the trailhead access directions and rides follow public access routes through private lands. Steer clear of any "No Trespassing" signs. Leave gates as you found them. Don't push your luck: many landowners have no sympathy for trespassers and any lack of respect gives all mountain bikers a bad name.

Many of the public access routes through mining country pass by mining remains that are actually on private property. If you stop to look or take pictures please don't disturb these sites. They can be easily viewed from the road or trail. Some of Colorado's ghost towns are not all that ghostly but support small populations. Be aware of this situation and refrain from disturbing any residents.

6. Help protect Colorado's mining heritage. Between the ravages of nature and people there aren't many historical sites left, and it's up to the visitors to these unique spots to preserve what remains. Colorado's mining relics are the only existing "windows" we have to our unique past and these outdoor museums need to be enjoyed without destruction.

All of these guidelines are practical and easy to implement. Responsible biking techniques, courtesy on the trail, and sensitivity toward the environment can help maintain a positive public attitude and support of backcountry use by mountain bikers.

Preparations and Precautions

When riding in the backcountry you need to be self-sufficient. Know your limitations, carry the necessary supplies, and be prepared to handle any type of situation that might arise.

Equipping yourself properly for a backcountry ride means always bringing a few essential items that can be strapped under your seat in a small bag or carried in a daypack, in a fanny pack, or on a rack. These necessities include:

• tire irons	• map	• high energy snacks
• spare tube	• compass	• sunscreen
• tube patch kit	• pocket knife	• sunglasses
• pump	• liquids	• clothing for inclement weather

Additional tools and accessories to consider are:
- 4-5-6 mm allen wrenches
- 6" crescent wrench
- 8-9-10 mm wrenches
- 1" strapping tape for tire rips
- small flat- and phillips-head screwdrivers
- matches
- first aid kit
- chain lubricant
- chain tool

A word on mountain biking attire: comfort is important. Bike in clothing that works for you. Always bring enough layers and protection to remain comfortable in changing weather conditions. Wear a helmet every time you ride. Even if you never plan to do any aggressive biking, a helmet should be a mandatory piece of your biking equipment.

Having the appropriate supplies is only the first step toward being prepared for a backcountry ride. Your safety in the mountains means planning a ride carefully. Keep in mind your physical condition, ability to adapt to high altitudes, and expertise on a mountain bike. Don't hesitate to try out a variety of terrain but be sensible about when you've reached your limits. Keep your capabilities in mind. Mountain biking can be a very demanding activity, especially in Colorado, where most of the routes are at elevations between 8,000 and 12,000 feet. Start out easy and work your way toward more difficult rides.

If you're unfamiliar with an area you've chosen to ride in, carry the suggested map for that ride. Always leave word with someone about your destination. A word of caution about riding around mining country: a lot of open mine shafts and pits as well as many unstable structures dot the terrain. Much of the excavating and building was done over one hundred years ago when there were no safety codes and engineering practices were hit or miss. The routes described in this book purposefully steer clear of any unsafe situations. However, venturing off designated roads and trails when biking in mining country is a hazardous practice. Do not explore, inspect, or get near any mining operations or old buildings. Not only are you probably trespassing, but also you are putting yourself in potentially dangerous situations. Mining country is riddled with tunnels and underground shafts that can cave in unexpectedly and old structures are extremely unstable. Observe all mining relics from a safe distance. The simplest approach is to stay on designated routes, ride safely, stay in control, and be observant.

Before riding make sure your bike is in good functioning condition to avoid needless mechanical problems while on the trail. This relates to rental bikes also. If you're renting, go for a quick spin on the bike to make sure everything is operating correctly before you take off on a ride.

Take care of yourself during the ride. Drink plenty of liquids. Wear sunscreen to shield your skin from the intense, high-altitude sun. Protect yourself during hunting season by wearing bright colors and being exceptionally cautious if you're riding well off the beaten path. If the route takes you above timberline, start early and carry adequate clothing for those infamous Colorado mountain storms that can catch you when you least expect it. Get in the habit of starting early in the day. Always keep an eye on the sky and remember that summer thunderstorms can move in very quickly, especially during July and August, when afternoon storms are the rule, not the exception. A few fluffy clouds can, within minutes, turn into a powerful, dangerous storm, which can make it extremely unsafe to be caught in an open area. Keep in mind escape routes down to cover when riding above timberline and don't begin miles of high alpine pedaling if a storm is looming. Remember that rain can suddenly change route conditions. A previously passive trail can turn into a technical challenge after a torrential downpour.

Being prepared with the proper equipment and using common sense when planning for and during rides should provide you with an exciting, enjoyable backcountry experience.

How to Use This Guide

The rides in this book are divided into four regions. Several historic districts are grouped into each region based on their geographic location. Every region includes an overview map that highlights towns, roadways, and landmarks and identifies approximate trailhead locations. A section highlighting additional rides is included at the end of each region.

The ride descriptions follow a set format. An information capsule gives a brief overview of each ride, listing important features that will tell you at a glance if the ride is appropriate for your ability. Detailed narrative is provided for the access, description, history, and comments sections. Also included with every ride description are a hill profile and topographic map. Below are brief explanations of these features.

LOCATION: Provides a general idea, in miles, of where the trailhead is, usually in relation to the nearest town. You'll notice that few of the rides actually start in the historic towns listed in each region. However, all of the rides can be done as day trips from these towns if they are your base locations.

DISTANCE: Approximate round-trip mileage is given for each ride. Since a cyclometer was used to record mileage, the distances are fairly accurate. Mileage is mentioned occasionally in the ride description to give you an idea of the distance you've covered. This can also be helpful when navigating, and distances are often given in reference to a distinct landmark or trail junction.

TIME: The estimated time is geared for the average rider and accounts for the hours needed, including short breaks, to complete a ride. Time varies greatly depending on the ability of a rider and his or her goals. You can determine if you fit within the given times or are consistently faster or slower after you have ridden a couple of the described routes. Keep in mind that the historical nature of these rides may cause a slower than usual pace.

RATING: Rating a backcountry road or trail for rideability is one of the hardest things for a mountain biker to do. Varied levels of competence and fitness make each mountain biker approach a route from a different perspective. Consequently, the ride ratings provide only a general idea of the difficulty of each ride. The difficulty level indicates what overall technical and physical abilities are needed to complete a ride. Ratings are based on the rideability of the road or trail and take into account obstacles such as loose rock, roots, and stream crossings. Also considered are the length of the ride, elevation gain and loss, and steepness of climbs (gradient).

EASY: Minimal biking experience and physical exertion are required. Routes contain very few technical obstacles. Climbs and descents are gradual. However, for someone not used to exercising at elevations above 8,000 feet, there are very few truly "easy" rides in Colorado. If you fit into this category and aren't acclimated to higher elevations you can still have a great backcountry biking experience. Just be prepared to take a little longer, rest more frequently, and maybe do some walking.

MODERATE: Requires a moderate level of physical effort. Some long, gradual or short, steep climbs occur. You must be capable of maneuvering your bike over some obstacles, such as loose rocks or small stream crossings. Walking your bike for short distances may be necessary.

MORE DIFFICULT: Good physical condition is necessary for riding up extended steep grades. Elevation gains can be considerable. You should have solid mountain biking skills and the technical ability to negotiate rocks, streams, bogs, ruts, etc. Some walking is likely.

ADVANCED: You need to be able to ride for extended periods over rough terrain. Routes require expert riding skills. Long climbs and extensive elevation gains demand top physical condition. Occasional hazardous route conditions require periods of walking.

Many ride ratings are a combination of two categories, for example, moderate-more difficult. Sometimes a ride starts out easy and progresses to an advanced rating, or it may be almost entirely moderate with one small section of advanced climbing in the middle. If a ride fits into this situation, an asterisk marks the rating that describes the majority of the ride, for example, easy*–more difficult. An explanation of the asterisk is provided at the end of the information capsule. Also, the comments section and ride description will elaborate on situations (usually a significant terrain change) that necessitate a different ride rating.

The ratings give you an idea of what to expect. You make your own decisions on what to attempt, using the rating only as a tool to help find a ride compatible with your ability. Read the entire description and experiment. Don't let longer distances scare you. Some of the longer rides have an easier rating due to a less strenuous level of rideability. Some short rides have more difficult ratings because of technical, strenuous riding. In addition, ratings apply only when taking the described trail direction. Following the direction opposite of the described route may alter the ratings. The ratings also are based on current road and trail conditions, which often change due to weather or human-made causes. Check with the Forest Service or local bike shops for an update on conditions.

Remember, mountain biking in the Colorado Rockies means climbing is frequently the norm and being out of breath is common. But it also means being surrounded by some of the most beautiful scenery on Earth. So when you find yourself stopping to catch your breath or walking your bike, don't forget to enjoy the columbines blooming along the road or the sheer cliffs glistening in front of you. That's what backcountry biking is all about.

LOW ELEVATION, HIGH POINT, ELEVATION GAIN: The lowest and highest elevations are given for each ride. The elevation gain gives the change in elevation between the lowest and highest point. You may experience additional smaller elevation gains and losses on rides that cover rolling terrain. These changes are usually insignificant and are not calculated into the figures given for the elevation gain.

TYPE: Each ride is classified either as a loop (riding in one direction with little or no backtracking) or as an out and back (riding out in one direction and then backtracking on the same route). Also included in this section is the ride's categorization as dirt road, single track (trail), or both. You are informed if the ride includes paved roads, which are used only when necessary to access a ride or complete a loop.

You'll notice that many of the rides in this book are roads, simply because they were developed as such one hundred years ago. However, this does not necessarily mean you can expect such rides to be heavily traveled jeep routes. Each road develops its own character. Many have deteriorated into overgrown, rarely used double tracks, others have become four-wheel-drive routes, and some are classified as county roads.

SEASON: The suggested time of the year gives you a general idea of when you can do a ride. Colorado's fickle weather makes it tough to predict exactly when mountain-bike season starts and ends. Snowstorms in May and June or sunny, dry weather in November can shorten or lengthen the biking season considerably. Generally, routes above 10,500 feet won't be bikeable until the middle of May. Above 11,000 feet biking season starts in June, with snowdrifts at even higher elevations and on northern exposures well into July. A ride listed as year-round may get snow, but it usually doesn't remain long. If in doubt about the snow conditions on a ride, ask a local.

MAPS: Trails Illustrated, National Forest, USGS County Series, and USGS 7.5 Series topographic maps are listed for the area covering each ride. Each of these maps has a different type of information and date of currency. The 7.5 Series are the most detailed, the National Forest cover the largest area, and the Trails Illustrated are usually the most recently updated. I use the Trails Illustrated maps whenever possible. Although they are not available for the whole state, they cover most of the regions toured in this book. Qualities including waterproofness, durability, detail, a symbol identifying bikeable routes, and continual revisions make Trails Illustrated maps excellent tools for mountain bikers.

The map included with each ride description is a portion of the USGS County Series 1:50,000. This series covers a large area and reduces well into book form. But many have not been updated recently and some of the side roads and trails mentioned in the descriptions are not shown on these maps. In addition, some routes shown on the topo maps will not correspond to what is actually in the backcountry. It's to your advantage to have some navigating ability, to be able to distinguish landmarks and elevation changes, and to know how to use these skills when reading a map. I strongly advise carrying a complete map of the region to supplement what the book provides.

HILL PROFILE: This graph combines elevation and distance statistics to give you an idea of the amount of ascent and descent within a ride. It shows whether elevation is gained or lost all at once or in series of ascents and descents. A topo map with 80-foot contour intervals was used to develop the graph. Minor elevation changes of less than 80 feet aren't shown. There are five profiles (Rides 19, 21, 24, 25, 28) whose mileage and/or elevation increments deviate from the standard.

ACCESS: Access descriptions provide directions on how to get to the trailhead using mileage and landmarks. All access routes can be driven in a two-wheel-drive vehicle. The described rides require only one car, unless you choose the shuttle options mentioned for some rides. Remember: signs, landmarks, road numbers, etc., may change, making some of the directions less accurate. Also, please park well off any roadway and away from private property or driveways.

DESCRIPTION: Detailed descriptions are given for each ride. I used landmarks and directions such as "right turn" or "left turn" as navigational aids. In addition, changes in terrain, side roads and trails, and distinctive natural features are mentioned to help you follow a route. Terminology frequently used includes the abbreviation for Forest Service (FS) and *cairn* (a pile of rocks used to mark a route). Read the entire description before attempting a ride. Details such as difficulty of climbs, traffic encountered, and when a ride changes from one rating to another are discussed. Of course, situations different from the described route are a possibility. Trail reroutings, washouts, road closures, or missing signs may change but will not completely hinder your ability to navigate. Road numbers, particularly Forest Service Roads, change frequently and may not correspond to the route numbers mentioned in the description. Patience, a willingness to explore, and a sense of humor are helpful qualities when route conditions are not what you expected.

HISTORY: This section includes a brief summary of the historic features you encounter as you ride. Some routes pass such a concentration of mines and sagging structures that it would take volumes to describe them all. Frequently I highlight only the most prominent sites. The bibliography lists several fascinating books that can further whet your historical thirst.

COMMENTS: Specifics on terrain changes pertaining to the ride rating are highlighted here. In addition, anything of particular importance or uniqueness, such as traffic, exposure above timberline, private property, car shuttles, and ride options, is detailed in this section.

ADDITIONAL RIDES: This section briefly summarizes more rides near the historic areas. I tried to include single-track options in this part as well as routes off the beaten path. Although many of these rides have little historical value, they are just too good to miss. The brief summary gives you an idea where the ride is located and what to expect. With a map and additional details from local bike shops or the Forest Service you'll find these rides an enriching supplement to the described historic routes.

BIKEABLE PASSES: Many of Colorado's high passes are perfect for mountain biking. The navigation involved when riding a pass is usually fairly straightforward, so these routes are listed without detailed directions. Many passes are best done as multiday trips or with a car shuttle. Biking most passes requires physical stamina and some technical riding skill, but there are a few mellow ones that novices will enjoy. The passes crossing between two regions are only listed once. I did not ride all of these passes and got much of the information on bikeable ones from locals.

* * *

Please use this guidebook only as a general reference on where to ride. All directions were accurate when the routes were last visited but changes do occur, especially around mining sites. Structures may collapse or disappear entirely. Fences and gates may appear across formerly open routes. I strongly recommend that you consult with local bike shops or the Forest Service about specific safety and route condition considerations before you go riding. Finally, do not use this guide as a substitute for your own good judgment. Take responsibility for making decisions about preparing adequately for a ride and choose routes within your ability. Most important, once you feel you've shopped, fixed, packed, read, and mapped yourself silly, go out there, hop on your bike, and have the time of your life!

Region 1
FRONT RANGE

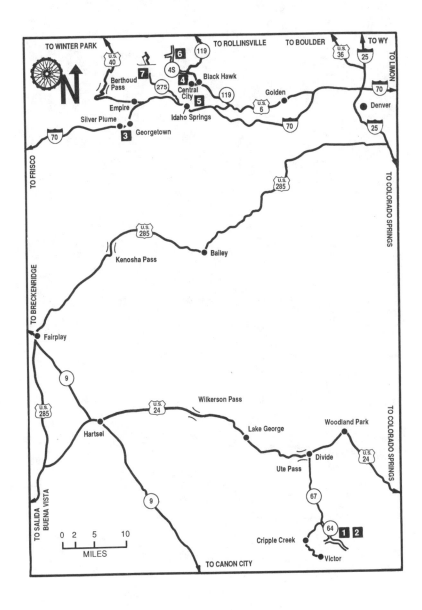

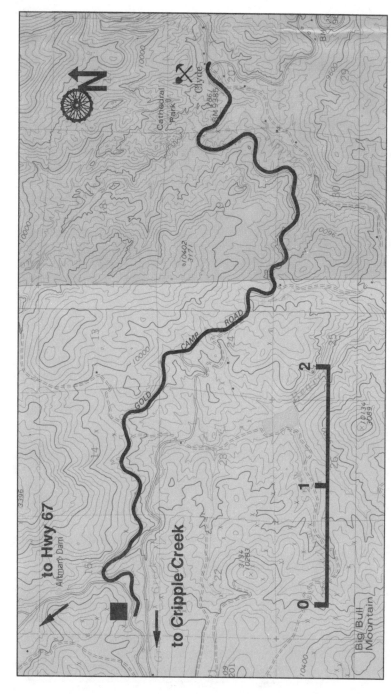

Rides Around Cripple Creek

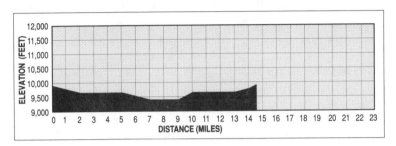

GOLD CAMP ROAD

1

Location: Cripple Creek
Distance: 14.5 miles
Time: 3 hours
Rating: Easy
Low Elevation: 9,440 feet
High Point: 9,840 feet
Elevation Gain: 400 feet
Type: Out and back; dirt road
Season: May–October

Maps
Trails Illustrated: none for this
    region
USFS: Pike
USGS County Series: Teller
USGS 7.5 Series: Big Bull Mountain

• • •

Following the Short Line Railroad grade, which traveled from Colorado Springs to Cripple Creek, the Gold Camp Road passes spectacular rock formations, cuts through narrow notches, and crosses above lush gulches with meandering streams and beaver ponds.

Access

From Divide, follow Hwy. 67 south toward Cripple Creek for about 15 miles. Turn left at a major intersection onto County Road 64 toward Victor. Follow this road for 3 miles as it turns to dirt and intersects the Gold Camp Road. Park in a large pullout on the left just before this intersection.

Ride 1   GOLD CAMP ROAD

Description

From the intersection, turn left onto Gold Camp Road. Descend gradually into groves of aspen and through the first of many narrow notches in the rock. (It must have taken some serious dynamite blasting in these areas to accommodate the train.) The road becomes nearly level and meanders among beautiful stands of aspen, across several drainages, and through many tight openings. Other than occasional washboard, the surface is quite smooth and seems made just for mountain bikes.

At about 5 miles you catch your first glimpse of Cathedral Park. These towering rock formations become even more impressive as you get nearer and eventually ride close to their base. During the light of midday you might be able to see different faces, called the Cathedral Masks, in the rock. I rode past this area in late afternoon when the setting sun lit the sheer cliffs in brilliant shades of rust and brown. Mountains in the Pikes Peak area dominate the distant skyline.

After approximately 6.5 miles of pedaling you pass through a tunnel, a novel experience but one to be cautious of because of limited visibility and the possibility of traffic. The sparsely populated area around Clyde comes into view on the left at a little over 7 miles. A couple private residences near a pond and a large open meadow mark the area that was once a railroad station and popular recreation spot. Just beyond the homes, FS Road 376 forks left. Some nice areas for a rest stop are just up this side road, and if you're not quite ready to turn around, the spur offers good opportunities for exploring.

This ride description turns around at Clyde. However, you can follow the Gold Camp Road all the way to Colorado Springs, where it eventually comes out on the southwest side of the city. Many people bike the entire road using a shuttle, since the total distance is over 30 miles.

When retracing your tracks you'll get a far-off perspective of the vastness of the mining around Cripple Creek. Although many towering mining structures have collapsed and the area has returned to a more natural state, several distinctive, mustard-colored tailings dumps still stand out quite a few miles before you reach your vehicle.

History

The Short Line was the third, and last, railroad to serve the Cripple Creek area, beginning service with two passenger trains daily in 1901. Its name came from the fact that it reached Cripple Creek in 9 fewer miles than the Midland train, which came from Divide. A popular tourist attraction, the Short Line created a competitive atmosphere, causing rates to drop to as low as 25 cents round trip at one time.

Paralleling the Gold Camp Road for much of its distance was a stage road, which originally was a trail around Cheyenne Mountain and was later established into a toll road. It lost the transportation battle when the Short Line opened but you might catch some glimpses of it if you look carefully to the south of Gold Camp Road. Most of the drainages you cross were originally spanned by trestles. Probably one of the most scenic was the bridge that crossed Bison Creek just before Cathedral Park. When the grade became a road, the trestles were removed and drainages were filled with dirt to provide passage for vehicles. The tunnel you pass through is the last of nine that were built on the Short Line. It is partially timbered inside for support, unlike some of the others, which were solid granite. These nine tunnels had a total length of 2,404 feet. Clyde, your turn-around point, was a stop for the train. A water tank stood near the road and originally a boxcar and tent were the station headquarters. Later, a few buildings cropped up and the lake below the road became a popular recreation area. Fishing, dancing, baseball, rifle shooting, boat riding, and refreshments were attractions for the tourists who came up on the train.

The Short Line ceased operation in 1920. The railroad grade was converted into a road and operated as a toll road until 1939. It then became the Gold Camp Road and was turned over for management by County and Forest Service personnel.

Comments

This is a well-known backcountry route to Cripple Creek and does get traffic. The majority of the road easily accommodates both bikes and cars, although caution needs to be taken in the narrow rock notches and tunnels. I've ridden this both on a Friday afternoon and on a Saturday morning. Each time I was so spellbound by the surrounding landscape I hardly noticed the few vehicles that passed by. Recommended riding times are early morning and late evening, avoiding holiday weekends. Fall is especially beautiful since large stands of aspen border much of the route. Ease of pedaling makes this a good family ride. Just be sure to choose an off-season time if riding with children.

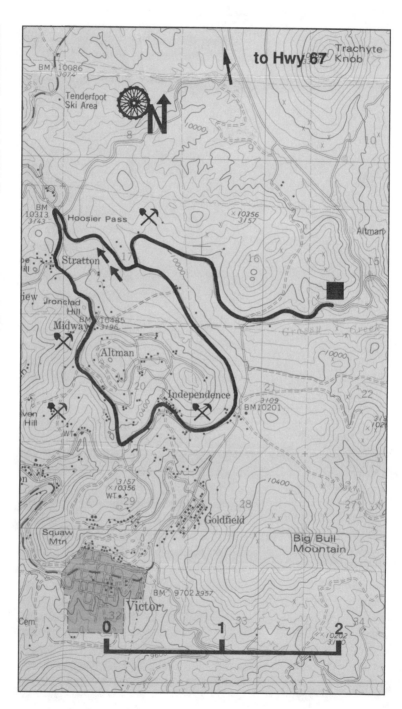

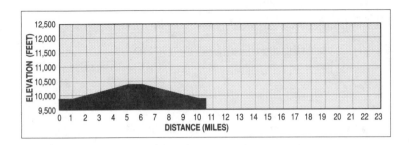

CRIPPLE CREEK

2

Location: Cripple Creek
Distance: 10.5 miles
Time: 2–3 hours
Rating: Easy
Low Elevation: 9,840 feet
High Point: 10,480 feet
Elevation Gain: 640 feet
Type: Out and back, loop; dirt road
Season: April–November

Maps
Trails Illustrated: none for this
    region
USFS: Pike
USGS County Series: Teller
USGS 7.5 Series: Cripple Creek N.,
    Cripple Creek S., Big Bull
    Mountain

• • •

Rangeview Road circles the hillsides east of Cripple Creek, passing many of the five hundred mines that once worked the area known as "the world's greatest gold camp." Sweeping views of the Continental Divide provide a spectacular backdrop to this historic tour.

Access

From Divide, follow Hwy. 67 south toward Cripple Creek for about 15 miles. Turn left at a major intersection onto County Road 64 toward Victor. Follow this road for 3 miles as it turns to dirt and intersects the Gold Camp Road. Park in a large pullout on the left just before this intersection.

Description

Begin pedaling up County Road 64 toward Victor and the hills above Cripple Creek. At this point you're on the Gold Camp Road. Originally the Short Line Railroad grade, it begins more than 30 miles east in Colorado Springs. A smooth surface makes this ride the "Cadillac" of dirt roads. There are no technical sections, so you can relax and concentrate on the unfolding historic scene.

As you get closer to the northern slope of Bull Hill and Bull Cliff, remains of many of the mines in this area are visible within thick stands of aspen. After about a mile of pedaling you encounter a three-way intersection. Turn right, continuing on the railroad grade, which climbs gradually through a large meadow. Prominent mines in this area are the School Section, on a hill across the road, and the Cameron, marked by large tailings slopes that spill into the meadow. Climb to the head of the meadow and curve left. Now home to placid cattle, this upper pasture once supported the popular recreational community of Cameron.

After almost 2.5 miles of pedaling you come to a three-way junction. Turn right and ride up through thick forests of aspen and pine. At the next three-way junction, to follow the described route turn left onto Rangeview Road. For a quick side trip, fork right and pedal up to the next junction, known as Hoosier Pass. Mountain views, a close-up glimpse of Hoosier Mine, and a peek down into Cripple Creek make this a good observation point.

Back at the junction for Rangeview Road you climb a more demanding grade past the currently operating Victor Mine. At a little over 4 miles descend into a small open area, where the town of Midway once stood. Its sagging saloon still exists (barely). Continue straight, passing a viewpoint on the right where you can stop and gaze at the Sangre de Cristo Mountains some 70 miles away. Ahead of you are extensive surface workings from the Cresson Mine. Below the road, clinging to the sides of Raven Hill, is a vast array of mining structures. Intense mining activity spilled into the gulch below, where the town of Elkton lay. Since this area contained some of the most productive ground in the district little was left undisturbed.

Continue to descend gradually. Watch high to your left for the headframe of the American Eagle, highest mine in the district. Drop to a three-way intersection and take the left fork (continuing straight here would take you on a steep descent to Victor). As you contour around the south side of Bull Hill you'll be overwhelmed by the amount of mining structures that crowd this hillside. Even in their abandoned state they portray a sense of intensity that must have permeated the area. Sitting just below the road are the sprawling remains of the Hull City Mine and dominating the far side of the gulch is the Vindicator operation. Scattered along the hillside above the road are a surprising number of well-preserved buildings that made up the community of Independence.

Curving left around Bull Hill you reach Victor Pass. Mountains dominate the view instead of mines, with Pikes Peak filling most of the horizon. Stay left at both intersections on the pass and continue veering left onto the east side of Bull Hill. This area seems quite removed from the furor of mining that took place on the other side. However, quite a few mines remain hidden from view. Only the red-tinted Cameron Mine, just below the road, appears through the trees. The loop part of the ride is finished when you encounter a familiar three-way intersection at roughly 8 miles. Turn right onto the railroad grade and backtrack to where your vehicle is parked.

History

To describe each historic structure encountered on this ride would take volumes. Consequently, only the dominant structures and critical historic locales are mentioned. Cameron, the first townsite you pedal through, remained one of the smaller settlements around the district. Starting out as a ranching community, it grew into a recreation center for the entire Cripple Creek region. A 30-acre amusement center called Pinnacle Park had dancing, a zoo, a playground, and an athletic field.

Midway, marked by the Grand View Saloon, was a favorite spot for miners to sit and drink while they waited for the next electric trolley to take them to or from work. It wasn't much of a town — only about 50 people lived here — but was really more of a passing through point for hundreds of miners who worked sites on Bull Hill.

Remains of several towns, including Anaconda, Elkton, and Eclipse, lie scattered along the hillside below the road as it nears the observation point. Elkton, one of the larger settlements, grew up around two huge mines in the area, the Elkton and the Cresson. A world-famous mine, the Cresson had a cavern of almost pure gold so valuable that a vault door was installed at its entrance. One chamber yielded $40,000 worth of gold in the first week. Elkton absorbed several nearby communities but most residents had moved on by the late 1920s.

Independence, the last townsite you encounter, never developed into the large commercial center it was expected to be. However, 1,500 people lived there by 1900 and some of the larger mines of the area developed around the town. The Vindicator, fourth largest producer in the district, recovered over $27 million worth of ore by 1951 and continued operating until 1959. Hull City Mine, located closer to town, produced almost $1 million by 1900. But water, a problem with so many mines in this area,

CRIPPLE CREEK

Ride 2

flooded the two lower levels and the mine eventually came under the control of the Vindicator. Independence is also known for the violence that occurred there during labor wars of the early 1900s. In addition to explosions in the mines, the Independence depot was blown up. Thirteen men were killed and many others were injured.

Comments

At times this is a popular driving route for people viewing the area's history. Weekends can be busy, especially around holidays. The road easily accommodates both vehicles and bikes, but to avoid a lot of the traffic ride earlier in the spring or in the fall. Or, try early mornings or late afternoons in the summer, avoiding the midday heat. Aspen thrive here, making this a superb fall tour. All mines and towns on this hill are easily viewed from the road. It is critical to remain on the described route. Private property boundaries are strictly enforced, with good reason: several current mining operations are in the area. Also, these hillsides are a maze of tunnels and shafts that can collapse unexpectedly.

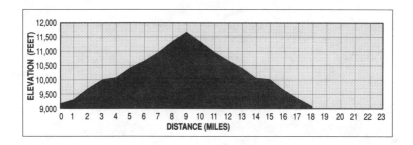

ARGENTINE CENTRAL RAILROAD GRADE

3

*Novices can bypass the single track and access the last 5 miles of the route, which climbs gradually over a well-defined road.

Location: Silver Plume
Distance: 18 miles
Time: 4–5 hours
Rating: Easy–moderate*
Low Elevation: 9,120 feet
High Point: 11,600 feet
Elevation Gain: 2,480 feet
Type: Out and back; dirt road, single track
Season: Mid-June–early October

Maps:
Trails Illustrated: Loveland Pass
USFS: Arapaho
USGS County Series: Clear Creek
USGS 7.5 Series: Georgetown, Grays Peak

• • •

The Argentine Central Railroad grade climbs gradually from Silver Plume over single track and dirt road to the crumbling remains of the Waldorf townsite. A high alpine valley and views to the Continental Divide reward riders who travel this historic byway.

Access

From Interstate 70 take Exit 226 into Silver Plume. Cross under the freeway. Turn right onto County Road 330 and pull into the designated parking area along the right side of the road.

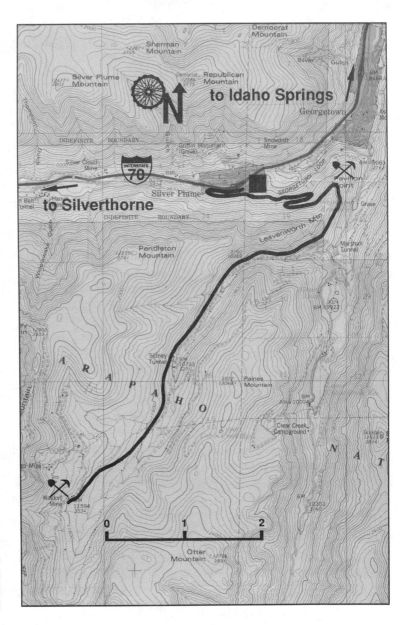

Description

The first 3.5 miles of this railroad grade alternate between dirt road and single track, are less maintained, and can be a navigational challenge. There are many spur roads and trails along the route and sometimes the most obvious forks aren't the ones you need to take. Try to stay on what seems like the gentle grade of a railroad. The single-track sections, although very gradual, are sometimes narrow and can be technical. Moderate biking skills are necessary. For those not comfortable with their trail skills, there is an option mentioned in the "Comments" section for reaching Waldorf.

Pedal 0.3 miles up the county road and turn left onto the railroad grade just before the road dead ends at a gate for a private residence. Follow this dirt road as it climbs gradually back toward Silver Plume. You reach the first major junction at a little over 1 mile. Pass a fork that switchbacks to the right and continue straight over a rocky section of single track and then back onto double track. You pass an interesting mine perched above the road on the right. At the three-way intersection soon after, marked by a nearby mine, switchback right. The next section becomes single track and passes old roads and trails taking off from both the right and the left of the trail. Negotiate several rocky sections and cross a small ravine that was spanned by a railroad trestle (remains of it are to the right). You may need to walk your bike here. Eventually you reach another switchback, which has a deceiving side trail that continues straight. Curve left onto the switchback and climb for a little less than a mile until you reach Pavilion Point overlook, marked by a stone chimney.

From here follow a road that curves right and continues climbing gently. Great scenery and impressive dropoffs enhance this segment of the grade. You reach a major three-way intersection at about 4 miles. Continue to the right on the railroad grade, now FS Road 248. (If you choose the shortened route suggested in the "Comments" section, this is where you connect with the railroad grade after ascending from Guanella Pass Road.)

The road climbs gradually but steadily above Leavenworth Creek for about 5 miles. The fairly smooth surface requires few technical skills. Aspen groves line the first couple of miles, but as you climb higher these are replaced by pines until you reach timberline, where mountains become the dominant feature. In front of you are some impressive peaks including Argentine Peak, the most prominent one, and Mt. Wilcox to the left, named after the creator of this railroad. The ruins of the Waldorf Mine, some railroad remains, and a couple of structures across the valley are all that remains of the mining activity in this area. The mines up here are privately owned; please enjoy them from a safe distance.

This description ends at Waldorf Mine but you have a few more options. Advanced riders can tackle 2 miles of steep, technical road that climb above the mine to Argentine Pass. Those wanting the views but not the challenging pedaling can leave their bikes and hike to the pass. You can also continue on the railroad grade. It switchbacks right near the Quonset hut, climbs for about 4 miles, and ends just short of the 13,587-foot summit of McClellan Mountain. Most of this route is quite bikeable although there are some rocky sections. Spur roads abound and a map is helpful in picking the route that follows the grade. Numerous campsites around Waldorf make this the ideal location for an overnight bike trip, which allows for more time to pursue the ride options. Keep in mind that these upper roads usually aren't clear of snow until early July.

History

Originally, before the opening of Loveland Pass, a wagon road over Argentine Pass provided a critical route for getting supplies down to the busy Snake River mining region in Summit County. The difficulty of transporting ore and materials from Silver Plume to the high mining camps prompted Edward Wilcox, owner of over 65 mines in the area, to build the Argentine Central Railroad, which opened in 1906. Wilcox was a very religious fellow and his train never ran on Sundays, which created quite a problem considering the train was as much of a tourist attraction as it was a necessity to the miners. The thrill of riding a train to a mountain summit that promised views of "one-sixth" of Colorado attracted many adventurers.

At the head of the valley, before the final climb to McClellan's summit, was the little company mining town of Waldorf. The usual boarding house, hotel, stables, and other assorted buildings developed as a population of around three hundred settled in the area. In addition to the money they made from tourists passing through on the train, these high mountain residents made quite a profit with silver ore that was recovered from 80 veins located throughout the surrounding mountains.

Making a profit, however, proved no easy task for the railroad, and after both tourist and mining activity dropped, the Argentine Central was abandoned in 1920. Waldorf became a true ghost town at this point and succumbed to a fire that destroyed the last habitable structure in the 1950s. The Quonset hut was built by a remaining miner who was working Santiago Mine on McClellan Mountain.

The sturdy stone chimney that stands at Pavilion Point is all that remains of a dance pavilion called Scenic City Camp. This last-ditch effort to attract the dwindling tourist market met with some success, enticing Front Range fun seekers to enjoy the pleasures of mountainside dining and dancing.

Comments

The single-track portion of this ride has the characteristic gentle pitch of a railroad grade, but due to some narrow sections and technical spots it is not appropriate for beginners. However, novices with some rides under their belt may want to try this as one of their first trails because of the minimal grade. Bikers choosing the option that shortens the distance and avoids the single track can exit at Georgetown. Drive 2.5 miles up Guanella Pass Road, and turn on FS Road 248 (near a chain-link fence). Follow FS Road 248 up four switchbacks and merge with the railroad grade at a three-way intersection. Park here, or at the previous switchback, and begin pedaling up the grade, following the last part of the description. You're above timberline at Waldorf and are quite exposed, so keep an eye out for ominous-looking clouds that may necessitate a quick descent to protected areas. Expect some vehicle traffic on the upper road. When following the lower portion of the grade, avoid any side roads or trails — many lead to private property.

The abandoned Argentine Central Railroad Grade winds its way toward the Continental Divide.

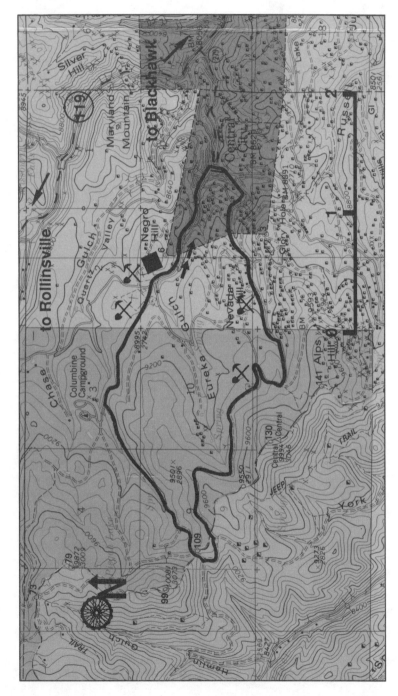

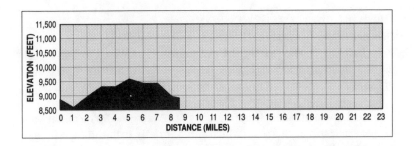

CEMETERY LOOP

Location: Central City
Distance: 8.5 miles
Time: 2–3 hours
Rating: Moderate
Low Elevation: 8,560 feet
High Point: 9,520 feet
Elevation Gain: 960 feet
Type: Loop; dirt road, pavement
Season: Late April–early November

Maps
Trails Illustrated: Rollins Pass
USFS: Arapaho
USGS County Series: Gilpin, Clear
    Creek
USGS 7.5 Series: Central City

• • •

This ideal half-day loop explores backcountry roads above Central City. Beautiful aspen groves, superb mountain vistas, and the opportunity to peek into this area's past via glimpses of its mining towns and cemeteries add to the variety of this ride.

Access
Once in Central City follow Lawrence Street (an alternating one-way and two-way street) as it climbs west through town. It turns to dirt about 0.5 miles beyond Central City and climbs a small hill. Park off the right side of the road in the pullout in front of a cemetery (across from the Boodle Mine).

Description

Descend on the main road back toward Central City. You pass a dilapidated stone building that housed the Rocky Mountain Brewery. Once you reach the downtown area, turn right at the stop sign and ride past a couple blocks of shops. Where the road splits by a parking lot take the right fork. Begin a moderate climb toward Nevadaville. After the road swings right you come to a spur marked by a sign that says "To Memorial." You might want to take a side trip up this road, which climbs briefly to the hilltop Masonic Cemetery. An overlook provides wide-ranging views of Central City and the surrounding hills.

Back on the main road you resume climbing. After a few rough spots the road smooths out as it climbs into the gulch and toward Nevadaville. There is a lot to look at as you pedal through this not-so-ghostly town. The road continues ascending along the base of Quartz Hill, which is almost completely covered with remains from heavy mining. After about 3.3 miles of riding, you reach a small saddle. Descend briefly through the trees to a four-way intersection. Make a sharp left and descend a bit more to Bald Mountain Cemetery.

Ride beyond the cemetery and through the fence onto FS Road 2732. The road contours around a hillside, passing through cool stands of pine. It contains a few rough sections but overall surface conditions are excellent, with little gradient change. There is a short climb to the high point, where majestic peaks near the Continental Divide slowly come into view. From this saddle descend gradually to an intersection at roughly 5.3 miles. Take the right fork. Continue to descend, hanging right at all forks. Eventually you'll merge onto a main road, marked as FS Road 175.

Descend a bit farther, following FS Road 175 toward the base of Mt. Pisgah, where you find an even better panorama of the Rockies and an intersection that has enough choices to confuse even an expert decision maker. Turn right onto a road that drops from view into a grove of aspen. This road splits a lot: always take the right fork and you'll be fine. All of these roads come together at the bottom. This half-mile descent is the most technical part of the ride. It has some moderately steep sections but remains completely bikeable.

You come out at the head of a peaceful valley. Turn right and descend along a fence. This is one of those almost-too-good-to-be-true aspen rides. The trees are thick here and put on an incredibly colorful show in the fall. Turn right at an intersection near the bottom of the drainage. This road shortly drops you onto a main artery where you turn right again. Follow this well-traveled road about a mile toward Central City. Pass by what looks like one large cemetery on your left. It is actually two separate burial grounds. The larger is the Catholic graveyard and a smaller one next to it is the Red Men Lodge Cemetery. Just beyond these cemeteries you merge with the main road from Central City. Your vehicle is just across the road.

After your ride, take a few moments to walk up the road that goes between the cemeteries you're parked near. Facing the burial grounds, see if you can identify the three separate graveyards. The Knights of Pythias site is on the left, with the city cemetery in the middle, and the small Foresters burial ground on the right. Farther up the hillside is a well-preserved mining structure. This blend of the pursuit of both final peace and prosperity intrigued me. It seems that no land around Central City was spared if there was a chance there was something valuable beneath it.

History

Quartz Hill, directly south across the gulch from Nevadaville, is the site of two major gold veins that led to the founding of this town. Both the Burroughs and Kansas Lodes were discovered in 1859 and were worked well into the early 1900s. Nevadaville is one of the oldest mining towns in Colorado and grew from quiet beginnings in 1859 to a boisterous population of 6,000 by 1864. It once threatened to become the largest community in the district, claiming one of the first schools, with 150 students, and 13 saloons. It even had a cricket club established by Cornish miners living in the area. A steady supply of ore from nearby mines kept the town going until World War II. However, its lack of water and its uneven terrain prevented it from ever achieving the importance of Central City. It did develop the reputation of being the winter sports capital of the region with the 2-mile downhill between the town and Central City being popular for sledding and early forms of downhill skiing. Quite a few buildings still remain on the main street. The easiest to identify is the two-story brick Masonic Temple on the left.

There were several major cemeteries around Central City. All were placed in beautiful locations, perhaps in an attempt to soften the common occurrence of death in this mining community. Although graveyards were positioned safely away from mining areas there are still stories floating around about caskets falling in on miners working in shafts below the burial grounds. These cemeteries reflect the hardships of life in a mining camp. Occupational dangers detailed on many headstone inscriptions mention explosions or other work-related accidents as the cause of death. Life in a mining camp was tough for the children, too, and a seemingly unfair number of graves are devoted to youngsters. Although quite a few elaborate headstones exist, simple unmarked graves are a common site. Many of the miners' widows had no money to pay for tombstones, and for some women it was the second or third husband they were burying because of the frequency of mining accidents. Some of the cemeteries, including the smaller Knights of Pythias, Red Men Lodge, Foresters, and Oddfellows were started as a benefit of membership in these organizations. If someone joined and bought the appropriate insurance, they were given a plot in that organization's cemetery.

Comments

You will experience some traffic for the first few miles before you turn off toward Bald Mountain Cemetery. Jeep drivers frequent the Forest Service roads, especially on weekends, but they travel slowly. There is quite a bit of private property in this area. It is well marked and easily avoidable by staying on the described route. This ride takes you into the core area between Idaho Springs and Central City, where several ride options exist. Using a well-marked map when exploring will help you identify public access roads amidst the privately owned land. The cemeteries are a critical part of this area's history. Some of them are still used and all need to be treated with respect.

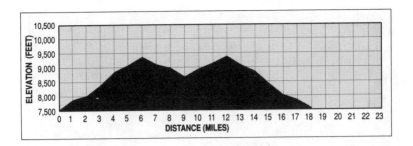

OH-MY-GOD
ROAD

5

Location: Idaho Springs
Distance: 18 miles
Time: 4–5 hours
Rating: Moderate
Low Elevation: 7,520 feet
High Point: 9,360 feet
Elevation Gain: 1,840 feet
Type: Out and back; dirt road,
    pavement
Season: All year

Maps
Trails Illustrated: Rollins Pass
USFS: Arapaho
USGS County Series: Clear Creek,
    Gilpin
USGS 7.5 Series: Idaho Springs,
    Central City

• • •

This famous and spectacular backcountry route travels from Idaho Springs to Central City. Carved into a steep mountainside, it climbs gradually through some of the most heavily mined country in Colorado. The combination of large doses of mining history, great views, and the chance for lunch at one of Central City's many eateries makes this a unique riding experience.

Access
From Interstate 70, take Exit 240 at Idaho Springs. Drive into town. Turn right on Colorado Boulevard and drive east through town. There's a small park on the left by the river where you can park.

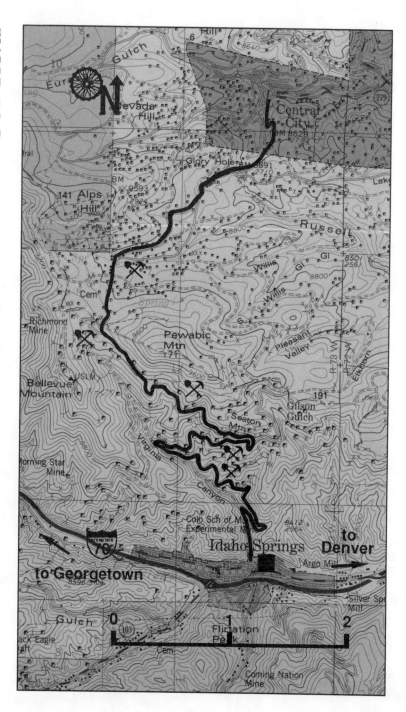

Description

Looking north from your car it's hard to believe there's a road carved into the steep terrain. But, that's where you're headed. Oh-My-God Road, often hidden from view, creatively snakes its way up the sides of Seaton and Pewabic mountains. From the park, take the first right onto 23rd Avenue and cross the bridge. Turn left onto Virginia Street, ride 0.4 miles, and turn right onto Canyon Road. Ride up Canyon Road. At about 1 mile, after you complete one of the steepest sections of the ride, the pavement ends. There's a three-way intersection. Take a sharp right onto a well-maintained dirt road.

This is the beginning of Oh-My-God Road. The road surface is excellent because of continual maintenance, but there is occasional washboard and gravel. Many side roads fork off this route toward private property, but the main road always remains obvious. Telltale signs of mining activity appear as you switchback up the canyon. Shafts, tailings slopes, and weathered structures in various states of collapse clutter the mountainside. At roughly 2.5 miles, just to the right of the road, is a weathered ore bin used by mines of the Idaho Tunnel.

At almost 3 miles you reach a major intersection. Hang a sharp right and continue climbing. Evidence of mining activity becomes more frequent in the next mile. Intermittent glimpses of snowcapped peaks, including unobstructed views of Mt. Evans adds to the visual distractions. If you stop to absorb the sights, be sure to pick a spot where you're visible to vehicular traffic and out of the way. At about 4 miles, on a hillside below the road, are the remaining buildings of Foxhall Tunnel, and above is the Seaton Mine, for which this mountain was named. A short distance up the road, just around a corner, is a major intersection. Take the left fork, which climbs for another 2 miles to the top. You continue to pass mining remains including the impressive wooden ore bin of the Comstock Mine, which clings to a steep slope just above the road on the right.

You reach the high point at approximately 6 miles and have a couple of options. If low on energy or time, you may want to turn back, returning the way you came. Or, you can continue to Central City. Follow the main road that drops down the other side of the saddle. Descend gradually into Russell Gulch, passing through what's left of the town at about 6.5 miles. There are some side roads in here; stick to the main route, which drops into the gulch and then curves right and slightly above it. The remaining structures in this area display an interesting blend of old and new. Ride at a leisurely pace to soak in the historic architecture and the impact of surrounding mining activity.

Continue descending, curving left and passing under the Colorado Chain-O-Mines operation. You turn a corner and catch your first glimpse

OH-MY-GOD ROAD

Ride 5

of Central City spread out below. From this point you get an interesting perspective of the surrounding mines, which look as if they attempted to creep down and consume the town. Arrive at Central City after about 9 miles of pedaling. If you time it right you can reach town in time for lunch. Retrace your route for the return trip. The first climb out of town is a little steep, but the road levels out quickly.

History

Oh-My-God Road was the major toll road between Idaho Springs and Central City. It was also the main road into Idaho Springs and the rest of Clear Creek County for many years. A critical route for miners who worked the hillsides above town, the road was used for hauling supplies up the mountain and bringing loaded ore wagons down. William Campbell, who surveyed and laid out the town of Idaho Springs, also engineered and built this road. It was basically a footpath the first few years but was widened to accommodate coaches and horses in 1865. Although used continuously from its opening until today, it lost much of its traffic once train service reached the mining settlements.

Both gold and silver came from mines scattered above and below the road. At the head of Virginia Canyon, between Idaho Springs and Central City, was a gold belt that accounted for numerous free-milling gold lodes. The majority of the lodes were small but quite rich with gold. On the eastern side of the mountain ran a silver belt. The Idaho Tunnel, located near the ore bin at the beginning of the ride, cut across six veins in Seaton Mountain and operated until 1935. One of the more valuable properties in this area, Seaton Mine, produced both gold and silver but had especially large amounts of silver. Its shaft was over 400 feet deep and accessed six levels. The Comstock Mine combines old with new. During its original years of operation it produced over $200,000 in both gold and silver ore. Above the old ore bin is a more recent metal headframe marking the shaft. Reopened and currently operating, the Comstock has been deepened in an attempt to uncover additional riches.

From the top, if you look down Virginia Canyon Road you see remains of a stone building. This is all that is left of the Williams Mine. The stone building held the hoist that was used to lower and raise men, materials, and ore from the nearby shaft.

Gold was discovered in Russell Gulch in 1859 by its namesake, William Green Russell, the man who started the Colorado gold rush with mineral discoveries around Denver. Russell Gulch reached its peak quickly, gaining 2,500 residents in a year, but dwindled just as quickly after placer gold ran out within four years. Lode mining continued and the town stabilized, for a time changing to profit-making from "liquid gold" during Prohibition. Deserted mine shafts were perfect warehouses for the bootleggers. The post office closed in 1943, but a few residents remain. Supposedly there's gold on the road from Russell Gulch down to Central City. Mine tailings were used in building this section and there's usually some ore left in these dumps, so perhaps you're dusting your tires with something more valuable than dirt.

Comments

Because of its exposure, this route holds very little snow, making it an excellent choice for warm winter days, early spring, and late fall. These are also the best times for avoiding traffic, which can be common on this ride. The road is wide, easily accommodating both bikes and cars, but use caution around the blind corners. Avoid midsummer (when it's too hot to ride anyway) and holiday weekends and you'll probably have the road almost to yourself. Although the grade on this route is gradual, the extended climb might make it challenging for novice bikers. An alternative more appropriate for beginners is to shuttle a car to Central City and ride only one way. This ride passes almost entirely through private property. Stay on the described route to avoid both unsafe mining remains and the possibility of trespassing.

The only remaining structure of the Williams Mine sits near the high point of the Oh-My-God ride.

Ride 6   Kingston Peak

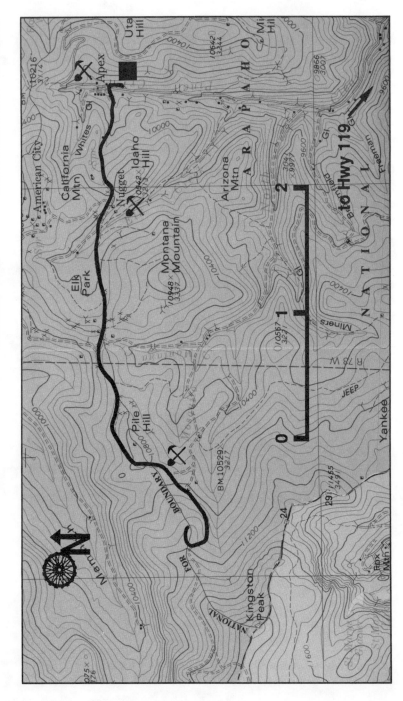

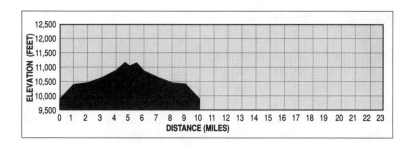

KINGSTON PEAK

6

Location: About 7 miles northwest of Central City
Distance: 10 miles
Time: 3 hours
Rating: More difficult
Low Elevation: 9,840 feet
High Point: 11,200 feet
Elevation Gain: 1,360 feet
Type: Out and back; dirt road
Season: Mid-June–October

Maps
Trails Illustrated: Rollins Pass
USFS: Arapaho, Roosevelt
USGS County Series: Gilpin
USGS 7.5 Series: Central City,
 Empire

• • •

Starting near the old main street of the forested community of Apex, this ride climbs through open meadows in Elk Park and to tundra-covered slopes near Kingston Peak. You pass remains of the mining settlements of Nugget and Kingston, both located in beautiful mountain settings.

Access

Drive 1.7 miles north of Blackhawk on Hwy. 119. Turn left onto unpaved County Road 4-S, which drops below the highway and winds along a creek. (You've missed the turn if you climb rapidly above and away from the drainage on the highway.) Follow this dirt road about 5 miles and look for a pullout on the right, next to a fence. Park here, making sure you are completely off the road. If you reach the old town of Apex, you've gone too far.

KINGSTON PEAK

Ride 6

Description

You might want to do a little bit of stretching before this ride. It starts with a pretty good climb that will definitely warm up your muscles if they aren't already. Pedal 0.2 miles up the road to an intersection marked by a sign. Take the left fork that heads west toward Elk Park and Tolland. You'll pass some of the remaining structures of Apex. Many of these buildings have been restored and turned into residences.This town has a nice feel to it and if treated with care can continue to grow old gracefully.

Begin a more difficult, 1-mile climb that's not overly technical but is definitely a low-gear grind. At the top of the hill you catch your first glimpse of massive James Peak gracing the skyline in the direction you're headed. Descend to a creek and into the high alpine openness of Elk Park. Off the road on your left is the last remaining cabin at Nugget. The mine behind it is fenced off and marked by private property signs. Cross the creek and pedal through Elk Park, climbing gradually to the next high point. Then descend through a fence to where the road switchbacks right at about 2.5 miles. Follow the road that forks left here and climbs along the north side of sparsely timbered Pile Hill. You can tell there's some extremely harsh weather at this elevation: the trees have a windblown and weatherbeaten appearance. Snowdrifts may be encountered on this section of road well into June.

After climbing gradually around the side of the hill you reach an intersection with fenced off private land to the south. Stay right and continue climbing. The views become more and more impressive as a growing number of peaks fill the skyline. A small cabin below the road on the right is one of the few remaining buildings on Pile Hill. This area was mined with some success and supported a few residents. Cross over a cattle guard and descend briefly, passing a small pond (it may be dry in late summer). You see a lot of tailings, some collapsed structures, and evidence of a fairly large mine on the hill. This is a good place to compare views of the forested mountains to the east with those of the craggy peaks in Rocky Mountain National Park.

There are quite a few spurs forking left in this area; stay right and follow the road that continues climbing along the slope of a hill. You're heading almost directly toward Kingston Peak at this point. This next section of road may have enormous snowdrifts that can keep you from completing the ride if you're up here in early June. As the climb becomes steeper, you curve to the right and onto a shoulder of Kingston Peak. At a junction where the main road forks left toward James Peak (see ride 7) and continues climbing, turn right and follow a road that is closed to motor vehicles. Ride a short distance out to a knoll and stop. The road descends farther but isn't worth following. Expansive views make this a great spot to linger over a long lunch. This is the turn-around point for the return journey over the same route.

History

Apex was definitely the hot spot of this region during the 1890s. Quite a few good mines operated within a 6-mile radius of town. It wasn't large as Colorado mining communities go, but it did have style. Hotels, a newspaper, a telephone system, and a post office were attractive features for the more than 1,000 residents. The most lucrative mine in the area, the Mackey, was almost abandoned early in its career, but when the owner finally gave up and set off dynamite to collapse the mine, he discovered the main vein of ore.

Nugget led a much more sedate existence and was always overshadowed by nearby American City, north of the Elk Park area. Although it wasn't far from two larger communities, in the middle of winter that little corner of Elk Park must have seemed like the end of the world. Nugget had one mine and very little else; the children went up to American City for school. Closed off to public access, American City lies just a few miles north of Nugget. Although not as prosperous as some of the other mining districts of Gilpin County, American City became the headquarters for quite a few mining companies. Its most important asset was probably its scenic location, and in 1911, American City was used as the setting for a motion picture company. Many of the old cabins are now utilized as summer residences.

Kingston was located somewhere in the Pile Hill area. It is one of those mystery towns about which little is known. In the late 1890s and early 1900s there were quite a few residences on the ridge running between Kingston Peak and Pile Hill, but most are gone. Other than the somewhat intact mine on the hillside, which is believed to be the London, only a few cabin foundations remain below the main junction. The tailings dumps that dot the hillsides give you an idea of the acreage covered in search of valuable ore. Kingston, basically a small work camp, relied on Apex for all of its supplies.

Comments

This is a popular backcountry route. Expect to encounter jeep and motorcycle traffic, particularly on the main road and mainly on weekends. Much of this ride is in exposed areas. You wouldn't want to be caught up here if the weather turns nasty.

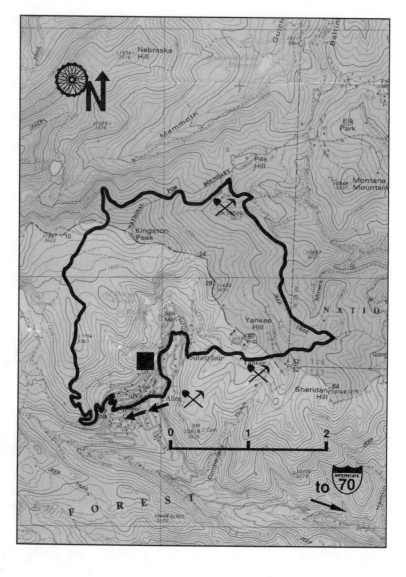

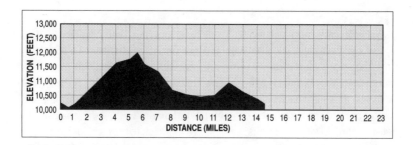

St. Mary's Glacier Loop

7

Location: About 8.5 miles northwest of Idaho Springs
Distance: 14.5 miles
Time: 5–6 hours
Rating: Advanced
Low Elevation: 10,080 feet
High Point: 12,000 feet
Elevation Gain: 1,920 feet
Type: Loop; dirt road, pavement
Season: Late June–September

Maps
Trails Illustrated: Rollins Pass
USFS: Arapaho, Roosevelt
USGS County Series: Clear Creek, Gilpin
USGS 7.5 Series: Central City, Empire

• • •

This classic high alpine ride climbs from the mining town of Alice, above timberline, around Kingston Peak and loops back toward St. Mary's Glacier on an old wagon road that crosses Yankee Hill. Jagged mountains, distant sparkling lakes, and a variety of riding terrain highlight this route.

Access

From Interstate 70 take Exit 238 (just west of Idaho Springs) for Fall River Road. Turn right onto Fall River Road and drive 8.5 miles toward St. Mary's Glacier. Park in the lot on the left just after the ski area.

ST. MARY'S GLACIER LOOP

Ride 7

Description

Ride back down the paved road 0.5 miles and turn right onto Alice Road. Pass a few old buildings and continue straight on Alice Road at the four-way intersection. A short distance farther turn sharply right onto a side road. Pass a couple of houses and take the first switchback to the left. This is the first of a series of switchbacks that carry you high above Alice. Shortly after, switchback to the right, then switchback left again. Follow this road southwest toward distant Mt. Evans; pass one switchback to the right and turn right onto the second switchback. Then take the next switchback left, heading southwest again. The road contours right around the hill as some great views begin to unfold. Beyond this point there are less spur roads to confuse you. Follow the route that continues switchbacking up the mountain.

As you ascend toward timberline the road becomes rockier and the climbs, more challenging. Walking for short distances is a possibility. Increasingly spectacular views of rugged cliffs and high alpine lakes make this difficult ascent worthwhile. After about 3.7 miles of climbing you reach the top of the toughest part of this ride. A small stone shelter provides a great windblock for a rest break. You definitely get that top-of-the-world feeling as you look down onto Loch Lomond Lake and its surrounding cirque.

Descend steeply along tundra-covered slopes (stay on the road to protect the fragile high alpine vegetation) and then climb again to the high point near Kingston Peak. This ascent is less abusive and much more rideable. You've pedaled roughly 5.5 miles by the time you reach the top. Mountains crowd the skyline in every direction with Longs Peak dominating the northern views. A challenging descent over steep, rock-filled terrain takes you to the James Peak Lake trailhead. If time and good weather are in your favor you may want to take a side trip to this beautiful lake.

The road switchbacks right and contours along the side of Kingston Peak. Smooth at first, the terrain becomes quite rocky as it descends to timberline, where a few roads converge. Follow the main road that curves right and drops into a drainage, where snowdrifts often linger into early July. They are usually small enough to walk through or around. Descend around a knoll and start looking on your right for remains of the small camp of Kingston and its surrounding mines.

You soon drop to a major three-way intersection at an open area marked by small mining pits and tailings dumps. You've ridden about 8 miles at this point. Turn right and descend farther, and then swing left by a burned-down cabin. Continue descending until you reach an intersection where a fork swings right and down into the forest. Take this side road and drop to a stream. Ford the stream and pass an odd accumulation of mining junk, including a roof without a house.

Contour along a hillside for the next couple of miles as you encounter small hills, alternating smooth and rocky terrain, and some stream crossings. The main road remains fairly obvious as it passes several enticing spurs you may want to explore at a later time. A short distance beyond the initial creek crossing, pass a spur ascending to the right. Hang left, staying on the main road. Near the top of a small hill pass through a fence and begin a short descent. Ride through three small creekbeds to a three-way junction after the third creek. Take the left fork, which proceeds straight into the trees. It climbs gradually over a rocky section of road to a small knoll. After some more descending and ascending you come to another knoll marked by small tailings dumps and faint spur roads. Descend on the main road a little bit farther and merge with FS Road 175 at approximately 11 miles. Turn right, descend briefly, and then start a tough but rideable climb up Yankee Hill on FS Road 175. Crest Yankee Hill after almost a mile of strenuous pedaling.

From the top descend briefly; hang right at a three-way intersection and stay on FS Road 175. You actually climb some more and then contour around the side of Yankee Hill through an area full of tree stumps and the sparse mining remains of Yankee. Superb views of St. Mary's Glacier appear before the final descent. Drop steeply and fork left at an intersection about halfway down where you see some condo rooftops. Shortly after, merge with a well-traveled dirt road. Turn right and follow this road past some residences. Continue descending to Silver Lake, where you access the paved road that takes you down to your vehicle.

History

Much of the route that you ride was heavily traveled by prospectors as they worked mines and moved supplies between Alice, Yankee, Kingston, and Central City. The entire basin below St. Mary's Glacier was populated and many claims existed although few were extensively developed. Alice was the largest community along Fall River. Placer gold was discovered in 1881, the Alice Mine was developed, and a large glory hole (just beyond where you take your first right to climb) was created. This enormous hole, dug in search of mineral-rich ore, measured 100 feet across and 50 feet deep. It's now mostly filled in. Mining camps come and go quickly and Alice was one of these. After Alice Mine closed, the residents moved on so quickly that the schoolteacher never received her final paycheck. In addition to its mining, Alice became an important stop on the stage road between Georgetown and Central City. Although you can see a few remains of Alice's original structures and there are a some mining frames on the hillside, most of the buildings are either gone or incorporated into summer residences.

Yankee, east of Alice and just below the top of Yankee Hill, was named during the Civil War by supporters of the North. The Forest Service road you follow up to Yankee Hill was once part of the same important stage route that stopped in Alice. There isn't much left of Yankee and you see very little from the road, mainly mining pits scattered among the barren hillside. Yankee's remote location made it a tough place to mine and little was produced in the area. At first the miners lived in tents. Then quite a few log cabins were erected, but the area never flourished. It only had one bar, an almost unheard-of occurrence in a mining town. After several years the residents eventually gave up after continually fighting bad weather and recovering only moderate gold-bearing ores.

About halfway through the ride you pass along a hillside that once supported an outpost type of camp, Kingston. As the crow flies, it wasn't far from the communities below the glacier, but it was almost entirely isolated during the winter. There was actually quite a bit of mining in this area as is evident by all the yellow tailings scars dotting the hillside.

Comments

You are above timberline for a long time and would not want to be caught up here in nasty weather since there is nowhere to seek shelter. Get an early start and plan this trip for a guaranteed good weather day. You may see a jeep now and then headed for the numerous hiking trails and interesting spur roads that you may want to explore later. Make sure to stay on the described route in the residential areas; these folks are awfully kind to let recreationalists pass by their homes.

ADDITIONAL RIDES IN
REGION 1

• • •

Mueller State Park

Mueller State Park encompasses a region crisscrossed with old ranch roads and game trails. Tentatively scheduled to open in the summer of 1991, this park will have approximately 20 miles of roads and trails open to mountain bikes. Dome Rock State Wildlife Area, bordering the southern edge of the park, contains many additional miles of road. Routes open to mountain bikes are strictly regulated and the process of identifying bikeable sections of Dome Rock is currently underway. A map and area regulations are posted at the parking area. Watch for closures in certain sections during late spring, which protect a herd of bighorn sheep during their lambing season. Magnificent rock outcrops, a variety of wildflowers, and cool forests of aspen and pine make this a unique environment to explore. Both Mueller and Dome Rock are accessed just a few miles south of Divide on Hwy. 67.

Beaver Creek Loop

This 16.5-mile, moderate–more difficult loop travels through forested areas and meadows south of Pikes Peak before climbing toward Mt. Baldy and then dropping behind its west side and into Middle Beaver Creek drainage. The first 7 miles follow Gold Camp Road east from Clyde to Rosemont Reservoir. The route then climbs along East Beaver Creek on FS Road 379 and toward Mt. Baldy. Taking a fork to the west drops you into the meadows of Deer and Elk Parks. A rarely used single track descends down a drainage on the western edge of these meadows and into Middle Beaver Creek, where FS Road 376 takes you back to the trailhead. Novice and intermediate riders will enjoy the first miles of pedaling along Gold Camp Road and into the meadows and can even choose a side trip up to Mt. Baldy. More experienced riders will be challenged by rocky terrain on the short section of single track connecting the loop. This area of Pikes Peak is great for setting up camp and spending a few days exploring various bikeable roads and trails.

Phantom Canyon-Shelf Road Loop

Take your toothbrush and credit card on this one. This 65-mile loop follows the old railroad grade from Victor down Phantom Canyon and into

Cañon City. The return climbs, via the Shelf Road, back to Cripple Creek. Only strong bikers could complete this in one day. However, breaking it into a two-day trip with a hotel overnight in Cañon City makes this a moderate ride. From Cripple Creek follow Hwy. 67 through Victor to access the beginning of Phantom Canyon Road. A 30-mile coast through the canyon brings you onto the flatlands near Cañon City. Use County Road 123 as an access route into town. To take the Shelf Road back to Cripple Creek, get on Fields Street one block west of Burger King. Fields climbs north out of town, through ranch lands, and eventually onto the Shelf Road. This road covers about 27 miles. Half of that is moderate climbing with a few steeper sections. Warning: it gets hot here in summer and Phantom Canyon can have a lot of traffic. To avoid both of these problems try this ride during the spring or fall.

Hamlin Gulch

The Hamlin Gulch jeep road, accessed about 3 miles up Fall River Road, offers some of the most varied mountain bike terrain around Idaho Springs. A suggested 11-mile, moderate–more difficult ride follows Hamlin Gulch Road as it climbs to a ridge. From here you turn left onto FS Road 175, a main artery in this area that stretches between Central City and St. Mary's Glacier. This road travels over rolling terrain around Mt. Pisgah, past Pisgah Lake, and to the head of Hamlin Gulch where a rarely traveled road forks left from FS Road 175 and contours along the heavily forested west side of Hamlin Gulch. It dead ends at a superb viewpoint. Be aware that there is some private land in this area, including much of the bottom of Hamlin Gulch. Most of these lands are well marked with signs.

Barbour Forks

Following Soda Creek Road southwest from Idaho Springs leads you to the Barbour Forks jeep road, a main artery into an area full of old roads, motorbike trails, and game trails. The hillside terrain offers countless moderate-advanced biking options. One short but challenging 6-mile loop follows both dirt road and single track. From the parking area near the beginning of the jeep road the route climbs, steeply at times, through one large meadow and three smaller ones. At the last small meadow look for a faint single track that starts on a small knoll to the west. This trail backtracks down the ridge, paralleling the jeep road as it descends through the trees, into open areas, and around rocky knobs. At one point you come out into one of the small meadows before swinging left and continuing to descend along a ridge above the jeep road. Eventually turning into an old road, the ride drops steeply down a grassy hillside and back onto the jeep road near the parking area. You can also access Barbour Forks and an equally explorable area above Devil's

Canyon by driving about 9.7 miles up Mt. Evans Road, where a Forest Service road branches left off the highway just above a large pullout. About half of the roads and trails in this region are not mapped, including the described single track. Talk to the folks at Chickenhead Sports in Idaho Springs for additional directions and ideas for exploring.

Mill Creek

Mill Creek is accessed from County Road 251, which starts in Empire and climbs to the north. After passing the old mines around North Empire, the route turns into a Forest Service road that leads into a rarely used area between Empire and Fall River Road. Once above North Empire, you follow FS Roads 171.2 and 183 up to a ridge where you connect with an old road that loops around Mill Creek. Follow this loop counterclockwise, crossing Mill Creek twice on both the lower and upper ends of the loop. You ride past secretive cabins tucked back into the trees, through hillside meadows, and below craggy peaks. Both rocky and smooth terrain exist on this more difficult, 11.5-mile ride that travels through one of the least explored regions around the Interstate 70 corridor.

Bikeable Passes

Two bikeable passes in Region 1 include Guanella and Jones. Jones travels north and Guanella takes you south, but they both explore beautiful mountain terrain.

Mount Silverheels dominates the skyline at the destination of the Crooked Creek–Trout Creek ride.

Region 2
East Central Colorado

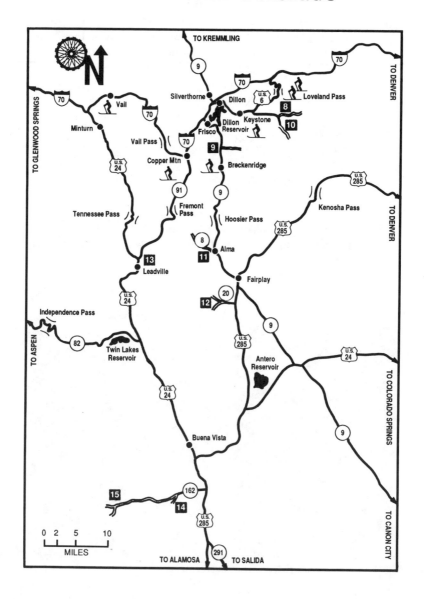

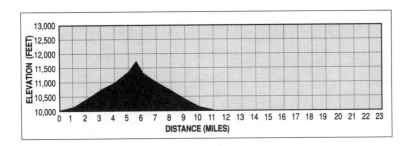

PERU CREEK

8

The majority of this ride is moderate. Beyond the Peruvian Mine the terrain becomes more challenging.

Location: About 6 miles east of Keystone
Distance: 11 miles
Time: 2–3 hours
Rating: Moderate*–more difficult
Low Elevation: 10,000 feet
High Point: 11,680 feet
Elevation Gain: 1,680 feet
Type: Out and back; dirt road
Season: June–early October

Maps
Trails Illustrated: Loveland Pass
USFS: Arapaho
USGS County Series: Summit 2
USGS 7.5 Series: Montezuma

• • •

The ride up historic Peru Creek Valley follows a jeep road past remains of many impressive mines. Climbing to timberline, this route ends at the base of a rugged mountain cirque containing more relics from the area's rich mining history.

Access

From Interstate 70 take Exit 205 for Hwy. 6 east and Dillon. Drive east on Hwy. 6 for 7.2 miles, passing through Keystone. Turn right onto Montezuma Road. Take the first left following the sign for Montezuma. Drive about 4.6 miles. Just after the road swings left and crosses the Snake River, turn left and park in the Peru Creek trailhead parking lot.

Ride 8 PERU CREEK

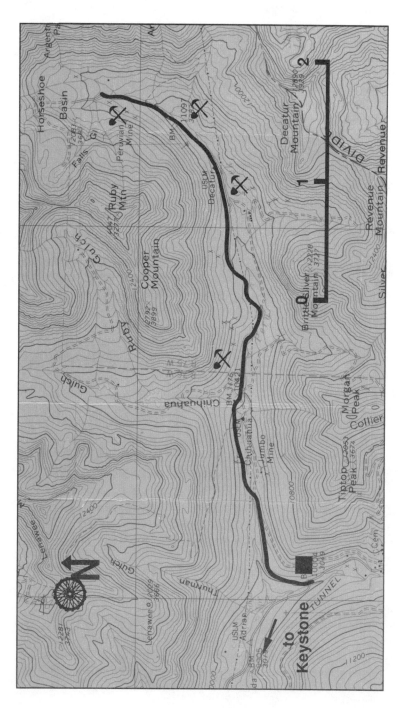

Description

From the trailhead, follow Peru Creek Road as it climbs gradually through forests of aspen and blue spruce, crosses Peru Creek, and continues up a moderate grade on the left side of the valley. Pass the Lenawee trailhead on the left at about 1.6 miles. This trail climbs steeply to the north, eventually ending at Arapahoe Basin Ski Area. The road climbs over a hill and down into an open area where the valley widens. Lenawee and Cooper mountains to the left and Collier Peak to the right dominate the skyline. The main road cuts through a small meadow, passing a fork to the right for Warden Gulch. A short distance later another road forks left and climbs into Chihuahua Gulch. At one time the thriving mining community of Chihuahua sprawled along the hillsides of this area. Now only a couple of decaying cabin foundations remain. After you leave the valley watch for a tombstone on the left at roughly 2.4 miles. It marks the grave of two young girls, Helen and Mary Clancy. You've passed it once you cross under the power lines.

You encounter steeper terrain as the road ascends along Peru Creek. This climb is short and the road soon levels out, crossing through a large hillside meadow that is filled with wildflowers during midsummer. You reach timberline and views become more expansive as the trees are left behind. Evidence from extensive mining activities dots the mountainsides on the right. Pennsylvania Mine, an extremely successful operation, dwarfs the other visible structures. Recent excavations around the mine are the result of a water quality improvement project.

Continuing on the main road, pass through a gate at approximately 3.8 miles. Argentine trailhead parking appears on the right at about 4.6 miles. Farther up the road this trail takes off to the right, switchbacks up to 13,207-foot Argentine Pass, and drops down the eastern side of the Continental Divide. Mountain bikers interested in riding Argentine Trail usually approach this challenging route from the more gradual eastern slope. Across the creek, on the hillside between Pennsylvania Mine and the trailhead parking, are a few crumbling remains of another mining community known by three different names: Decatur, Rathbone, and Argentine.

The road curves left near Peruvian Mine, which clings to a rocky slope just above the road. Beyond this point the route becomes more technically challenging as it climbs steeply into Horseshoe Basin, an impressive high alpine cirque scattered with mining remains. You can continue riding or explore the area on foot. A pleasant downhill cruise brings you quickly back to your vehicle.

History

Chihuahua, founded in 1880, was a prosperous silver camp. The energy and activity generated in this community livened the days of many hardworking

PERU CREEK

Ride 8

inhabitants in Peru Creek Valley. By 1881, 50 buildings existed including hotels, restaurants, saloons, and a sawmill. A small but vibrant town of around 200 residents, Chihuahua enjoyed occasional dances and social get-togethers with neighboring settlements and boasted proudly of its school, which had a peak population of 24 students during 1881–1882. A forest fire destroyed most of the business section in 1889 and little rebuilding was done. It's difficult to now find any remains of this once bustling community.

During the mining era a common practice involved the use of natural stones to mark gravesites. Death was such a frequent occurrence that many had neither the time nor money to order expensive gravestones. Years later relatives would often upgrade and re-mark these primitive sites using purchased gravestones. This may have been the case with the roadside graves of Helen and Mary Clancy, who perhaps were residents of Chihuahua. The cause of their deaths remains unknown, yet someone, possibly a more recent family member, has put effort into improving their resting place.

One of the more productive mines in Peru Creek Valley was the massive Pennsylvania Mine. Opened in 1879, the Pennsylvania operated continuously until the 1940s. Production peaked in 1893 when the mine produced almost $400,000 of silver. A network of six underground levels, dug in search of ore, made up the bulk of this extensive operation. Pennsylvania Mine remains well preserved even after the 1977 fire that destroyed the assay office, bunkhouse, and cookhouse/dining hall.

A hardy group of residents lived beneath soaring peaks of the Continental Divide, inhabiting a high alpine community famous for its numerous name changes. Originally called Decatur after its founder Commodore Stephen Decatur, the town got off to a slow start, struggling with an inaccessible location and the lack of rich-grade ore from nearby mines. The discovery of Pennsylvania Mine created a boom in Decatur, which, after closing and reopening its post office, changed its name to Rathbone. Unfortunately, a devastating avalanche smashed Rathbone to splinters in 1899. By 1900, a surge in mining operations provided incentive to rebuild the town. This time it was named Argentine after the nearby pass.

The Peruvian Mine, which looms above the road at the mouth of Horseshoe Basin, was a successful producer of both silver and lead. Gassy Thompson, a famous Summit County swindler, implemented one of his more creative scams near this mine. He was hired to dig a 100-foot underground passage into Ruby Mountain. After realizing the enormity of the task, he instead built a tunnel out from the mountain. Snow fell and covered the timbers he erected, and the "tunnel" appeared impressive enough to please investors who inspected the operation and paid Thompson. By the time the snows melted to reveal the nonexistent tunnel, Thompson had fled.

Comments

Branching off from Peru Creek Road are some interesting spurs worth exploring if you have additional time. Just be respectful of any "No Trespassing" signs. These are seen mainly in the lower half of the valley, which contains a lot of private property. The final section of this ride is above timberline, so be prepared for weather changes. Expect some vehicles on weekends.

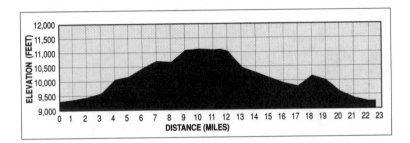

GOLDEN HORSESHOE

9

Location: About 3 miles north of Breckenridge
Distance: 22.5 miles
Time: 5 hours
Rating: Moderate–more difficult
Low Elevation: 9,280 feet
High Point: 11,120 feet
Elevation Gain: 1,840 feet
Type: Out and back, loop; dirt road, single track, paved bike path
Season: June–October

Maps

Trails Illustrated: Breckenridge South, Vail Pass
USFS: Arapaho
USGS County Series: Summit 2
USGS 7.5 Series: Frisco, Breckenridge, Boreas Pass

• • •

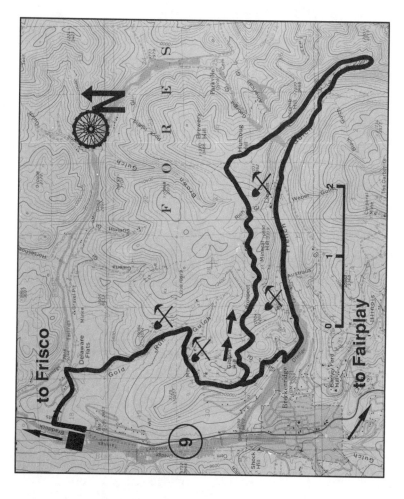

The Golden Horseshoe ride takes you into an area crisscrossed with roads and trails and full of old cabins and remains left over from the days when this region was a flurry of mining activity.

Access
Drive 2.7 miles north of Breckenridge on Hwy. 9. Turn left onto County Road 400 and park in a pullout by the bikepath rest stop (near a flagpole).

Description
Pedal about 0.5 miles down the paved bikepath. Cross the highway and turn right onto Tiger Road (by the Breckenridge Golf Course). Ride almost a mile and turn right onto Gold Run Road, which winds up along the left side of the golf course (watch out for wayward golfballs).

The road begins to climb as it veers away from the course and into the trees. At about 3 miles you ford a stream and pass the huge Jessie Mine stamp mill, which was used to crush ore. Curve right at the switchback and climb around the side of Gibson Hill. More mining remains and other collapsed structures marking the Preston townsite come into view. Veer left on the main road, continuing straight at a four-way intersection and climbing to the crest of Gibson Hill at almost 4.5 miles. Contour along an aspen-covered hillside and continue straight at a four-way intersection marked by a private driveway on the left.

As the road begins descending look for FS Road 253, a main-looking road that forks left. Turn here and climb a short, steep hill. Follow the main road, which curves left and winds through the trees. The next few miles have a lot of spurs branching off; the described route remains fairly obvious. At a three-way intersection turn right. Pass some faint spurs that head down, and turn left at the next intersection. (There's a lot of exploring in this area. Ask a local bike shop for more ideas on where to ride.) Climb gradually to a large turn-around with expansive views of Breckenridge Ski Area and the Ten Mile Range. Pass a spur that climbs left and continue on the main road, which descends briefly and then swings left. Pass some spurs forking right and climb a rocky section of road. Pedal by a small tailings pile on the left and continue climbing steadily along technical sections of road for over 0.5 miles. Crest Prospect Hill at a little over 6 miles.

You're now on the road that follows the rolling terrain of Golden Horseshoe Ridge. From Prospect Hill descend, continuing straight at each fork. Climb Mineral Hill. You pass an old cabin on the right and reach the top at just over 7 miles. Pass another cabin on the left. Descend on the main road as it switchbacks to the right and passes more mining remains on the

RIDE 9 · GOLDEN HORSESHOE

left. At a junction near a tailings pile, take the right fork, which descends into the tree-fringed meadow of Lincoln Park. Guyot and Bald mountains dominate the southern skyline.

Ride through the meadow, crossing two drainages and veering left into the trees. Climb steadily up a steeper grade for over a mile. This section may contain snowdrifts in early June. You eventually climb to a four-way intersection near an old cabin. Turn right for one last climb to a saddle on Humbug Hill. You'll pedal out to a five-way intersection at about 9.7 miles. A spectacular 360-degree panorama unfolds providing intimate views of Summit County's peaks.

From the choice of roads branching off from this saddle, take the one that climbs steeply up Farncomb Hill. Follow it a short distance, looking for a mining pit on the left. Turn sharply right across the road from the pit onto a trail starting near a timbered mine pit. Actually an old flume bed that brought water to the mines on Humbug Hill, this narrow trail contours along the steep hillside. It eventually connects with a wider trail, which follows near and on a ditch and continues along the right side of the hill. Some rocky sections and areas where the slope drops away steeply make this a technical challenge tempered only by minimal elevation changes.

Eventually you come out in Little French Gulch near the base of Mt. Guyot. The flume fades away and you'll need to cross a creek and turn right onto an old road. Descend past some cabins, following this abusively rocky road down the drainage until it connects with the well-traveled French Gulch Road at roughly 12.5 miles. You'll appreciate the smoothness of the maintained county road after the rough ride you just completed. Turn right and descend above the right side of French Creek. Heavy mining activity in this gulch is evident as you pass large tailings slopes spilling down the mountainside, a few lived in buildings marking the Lincoln townsite, the large Wellington Mine shrouded in aspen above the right side of the road, and numerous piles of rock deposited by dredge boats that scoured this drainage for gold.

Ride through an area marked by large orange-colored tailings and curve right on the main road. Look for a road forking right just past a couple of private driveways. You've missed it if you reach a major junction on the county road. Turn right onto this less traveled road and climb into a large grove of aspen that blankets the entire hillside. The road switchbacks left, passes a road forking to the right, and continues to ascend a series of short, steep pitches combined with some level stretches. You're back on the road you used initially to access the Golden Horseshoe area and you should recognize some familiar sites. Beyond the top of Gibson Hill you have a fun downhill cruise past Preston, Jessie Mill, and the golf course. At Tiger Road turn left and continue retracing the route until you reach your vehicle.

History

The Golden Horseshoe area is bordered by two of the most productive mineral drainages in Summit County. Many mines, cabins, and a few small communities lie in this region. One of the most impressive mining structures remaining in the county is the Jessie Mine stamp mill. Many mines opened in the area after the discovery of gold in 1859, but the Jessie Mine was the shining star. Producing low grade gold and silver ore, it operated steadily until 1909 and off and on again through 1936. The weathered giant that still stands is the 40-stamp mill. Some of the most amazing construction feats are hidden from view. A huge network of tunnels, one over 2,000 feet long, burrows through the hillside. Entrances have been collapsed to prevent entry into these dangerous openings.

Farther up the road, the first evidence of the intense mining on Gibson Hill is the decaying millsite of the Extension Mine and the nearby Oliver Filter. This large cylinder-shaped object was used for removing water from gold sludge. Around the corner, collapsed buildings are all that remain of Preston, a fairly active community that was once large enough to warrant a dress-making shop. Developed initially after the discovery of gold at the nearby Jumbo Mine, Preston was headquarters for three mining companies.

French Gulch, rich with valuable ore, was worked relentlessly by miners flocking to the area. Lincoln was one of the larger communities and swelled to a population of over 1,500 after a high quality type of gold was found nearby. The town declined after the crash of 1893 and only a few structures, most of which have lost their original appearance due to remodeling, remain standing along the side of the road.

Wellington Mine, clinging to the slopes above the road, had a long and successful mining career beginning in 1887. Producing lead, zinc, gold, and silver until 1973 it gained a reputation as being one of the area's most profitable operations. Additions of tunnels, larger shafts, and nearby mills all added to the Wellington's production capacity. It is believed that this mine had production figures of around $32 million.

Comments

Although solid physical and technical skill is needed to complete this route a rider with minimal experience can make it to the Preston townsite. Following the directions can be a navigational challenge due to the frequency of side roads (which often lead to private property and should be avoided). Expect traffic on the few miles of county road through French Gulch.

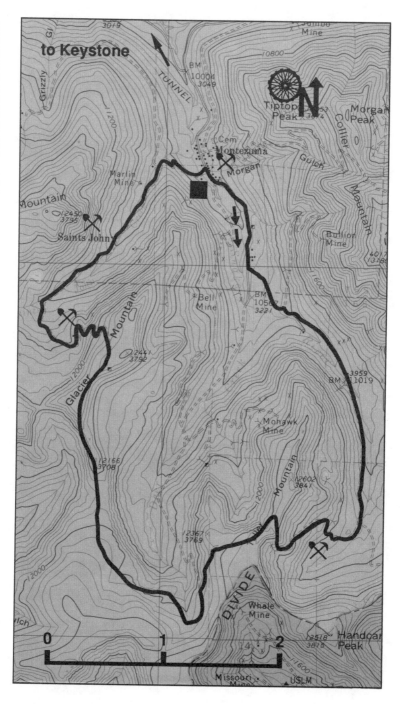

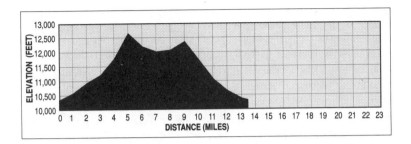

MONTEZUMA
LOOP

10

Location: About 6 miles east of Keystone
Distance: 13.5 miles
Time: 5–6 hours
Rating: Advanced
Low Elevation: 10,300 feet
High Point: 12,615 feet
Elevation Gain: 2,315 feet
Type: Loop; dirt road
Season: July–September

Maps
Trails Illustrated: Loveland Pass
USFS: Arapaho
USGS County Series: Summit 2
USGS 7.5 Series: Montezuma, Keystone

• • •

Riders tackling the steep terrain of some of Summit County's highest peaks are rewarded with peak-filled vistas and ridgetop riding along tundra-covered mountain slopes.

Access
From Interstate 70 take Exit 205 for Hwy. 6 east and Dillon. Drive east on Hwy. 6 for 7.2 miles, passing through Keystone. Turn right onto Montezuma Road. Take the first left following the sign to Montezuma. Drive 5.5 miles into Montezuma and park in a large pullout near a spur that forks right for Sts. John.

Description

Begin riding up the well-maintained Montezuma Road. After about 1 mile of pedaling look for a fork to the left marked by a sign for Webster Pass. Turn onto this rough jeep road and begin climbing, picking your way through loose rock and past several spur roads that lead to private homes and old mines. Pass through a Forest Service gate at around 1.5 miles and ride into a willow-filled meadow just below timberline. Ford the Snake River and pedal along the right side of the valley, following a rough, technical section of road.

At just over 3.5 miles you pass a fork to the left marked by a sign for Webster Pass. Another good ride, this spur climbs moderately to Webster Pass and the Continental Divide. For now, continue straight on the road leading to Deer Creek. It curves to the right and impressive views of a rugged headwall appear. Your technical and physical ability are put to the test as the road gets progressively steeper and more rocky and you climb the beginning of what is locally known as Radical Hill. A flat spot near the only remaining structure of the Cashier Mine provides a welcome rest where you can gaze at unfolding views of the surrounding peaks.

Beyond the mine the road continues to switchback up Teller Mountain. The road is rideable at first, but the steep pitch and rough terrain eventually require walking. I encountered snowdrifts in this upper section in early July, but they were easy to walk around. The view from the top of Teller Mountain (and for the next few miles of riding) makes the final steep ascent worthwhile. Although the mountain slopes around here are rugged, the summits are relatively flat and there's plenty of room to spread out and appreciate the top-of-the-world feeling that the miles and miles of peak-filled views provide.

Continue on the road as it descends toward Deer Creek drainage. At the first junction, turn left and descend a short distance farther until the road merges with another road that traverses the upper edge of Deer Creek drainage. A right turn here takes you down Deer Creek and quickly back to Montezuma, an easy out if the weather turns bad or you're short on time. To continue the described route turn left and climb above the drainage to a three-way junction marked by a sign. Turn right and follow this ridgetop road toward Sts. John.

The next few miles are exhilarating pedaling, characterized by mountaintop riding with bird's-eye views into the various drainages that originate in this area. Short steep climbs and technical descents will challenge your riding skills, and as you get closer to Glacier Mountain you'll encounter several steep pitches that require short periods of walking. You pass a couple of spur roads but the main route remains obvious.

After a final steep ascent the road curves to the right and you see General Teller Mine perched precariously on the edge of Glacier Mountain. Follow the main road as it climbs quickly over the ridge and descends into Sts. John drainage. A tricky, rock-filled descent brings you to treeline and past cabins and mining remains of the Wild Irishman operation. Continue descending on the main road as it winds down into the valley. At approximately 12 miles the buildings of Sts. John come into view. Cross Sts. John Creek and ride past both collapsed and restored structures. The last couple of miles you pass quite a few spur roads but the main route is easy to follow as it descends along the creek and switchbacks down to Montezuma, ending near your vehicle.

History

The founding of Montezuma was a result of silver discovered in the area during the 1860s. As word of rich claims attracted the usual fortune seekers Montezuma grew, slowly at first due to its inaccessible location, but eventually reaching a peak population of nearly 800 people by 1890. The usual hotels, post office, schools, and stores appeared. A drop in silver prices and several fires caused the town to struggle for survival. The post office finally closed in 1972, but a few full-time residents still inhabit this mountain community.

Mines line many of the mountain slopes above Montezuma and into the Snake River Valley. The Cashier Mine, which you pass as you climb Radical Hill, was often called "one of the best paying mines in the county." Discovered in 1870, its three silver veins were worked until the 1890s. Over 2,000 feet of tunnels were bored to access the ore.

Probably the busiest part of the Snake River Valley was the road leading from Webster Pass down into Montezuma. The opening of this route, originally a toll road, in 1879 caused much rejoicing in Montezuma and the town flourished with its new, easier access to supplies and the Denver ore markets.

The Sts. John drainage was also laden with rich ore and many mines are carved into both sides of this valley. The Wild Irishman, high on the side of Glacier Mountain, produced high-grade silver ore and supported a small community made up of several cabins that was never quite enough to become an incorporated town. Sts. John, farther down the creek, grew up around what is often referred to as the first silver strike in Colorado, which was made in 1863. The enormity of the Sts. John Mine, even in its current state of collapse, is evident from the remains stretching up the hillside. All that remains of the smelter, one of the first in the state, is a brick smokestack. The community grew into a company town of the Boston Silver Mining Association and boasted many amenities, including a 300-volume library. Some of the remaining buildings are being restored by the United States Backcountry Association, which rents them to backcountry visitors in both summer and winter.

Comments

Choose a guaranteed good weather day if you want to complete this ride. Much of it is above timberline and has no cover for waiting out storms. Above timberline stay on the marked routes to avoid damage to the fragile high alpine vegetation. You may encounter four-wheel-drive traffic, especially on weekends. Property owners in the area ask that you remain on designated routes and respect the "No Trespassing" signs.

Rides Around Fairplay

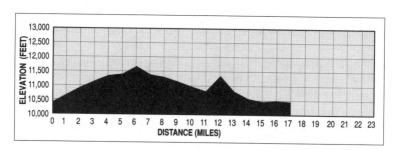

ALMA LOOP

11

The road up to Mineral Park is easy pedaling. Beyond Mineral Park and up and over the ridge to Park City the route contains terrain requiring moderate biking skills.

Location: Alma
Distance: 17 miles
Time: 3–4 hours
Rating: Easy*–moderate
Low Elevation: 10,400 feet
High Point: 11,640 feet
Elevation Gain: 1,240 feet
Type: Out and back, loop; dirt road
Season: June–October

Maps
Trails Illustrated: Breckenridge
   South
USFS: Pike
USGS County Series: Park 1
USGS 7.5 Series: Alma

• • •

This ride of contrasts travels from windblown timberline slopes where only bristlecone pine can survive to lush green forests of aspen. Bikers pass many of the mines and townsites that made up the mining district around Alma.

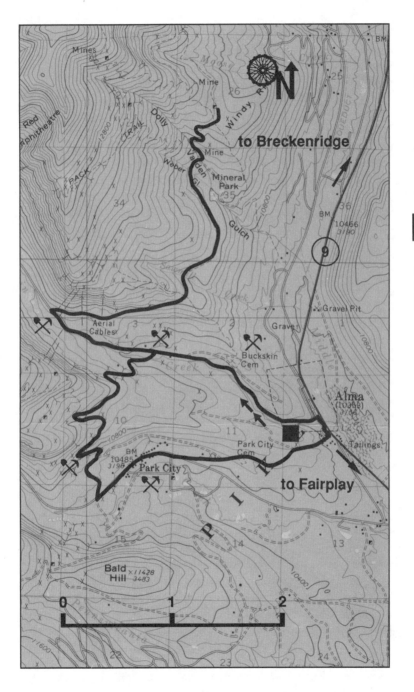

Access

From Fairplay drive north on Hwy. 9 to Alma. Turn left onto County Road 8, which starts in the middle of town across from a gas station. Drive 0.4 miles and park on the left in a large pullout above the creek.

Description

Follow the county road up Buckskin Gulch, which is dominated by the huge wall created by the Mosquito Range at the upper end of the drainage. After a little over 0.5 miles of riding there's a road forking right by a historic tour sign marked with an "A." Turn here and follow this road up into the trees for a short side trip to Buckskin Cemetery, which still serves the Alma area. Graves lie scattered along the forested hillside.

Back on the main road you'll notice leftovers from the mining era dotting both sides of the gulch. The town of Buckskin Joe, identified by a historic tour sign with a "B," occupied both sides of the road about 50 yards beyond the spur to the cemetery. A large tailings dump from Buckskin Joe Mine peeks through the trees on the left hillside. As you round the corner a Forest Service sign marks the site of a "primitive ore crusher." Look across the road by the creek for this bowl-shaped device, called an *arrastra*. A horizontal pole was used to drag heavy, rounded stones in a circle, crushing the ore. Water washed away lighter particles of stone and left behind the heavier gold-bearing material. Beyond the *arrastra*, bear right at a junction and climb past the hulking remains of the Paris Mill. Look across the creek to a distinctive cliffband on Loveland Mountain to see the clinging remnants of buildings that housed a terminal for an aerial tram that transported ore from mountainside mines to the road below.

At 2.5 miles, just past the Paris Mill, there's a fork to the right marked by a sign for Windy Ridge. Follow this side road as it climbs gradually, doubles back to the east, and passes a pond on the left. A glance up the steep mountainside reveals a few mining remains that refuse to relinquish their hold on the sheer cliffs. Yellowish tailings and dilapidated cabins are evidence of quite a bit of mining along this hillside. Views opening up toward South Park make you realize you're gaining elevation although it's barely noticeable because the road is so smooth and the grade so gradual.

The road eventually swings north and climbs gradually through the trees and into Mineral Park. A mine and some rundown cabins still stand. Above Mineral Park a junction marks the change from easy to moderate riding. Follow the right fork across Dolly Varden Creek and pedal over a short, steep section that will challenge even intermediate riders. Novices may need to push their bikes for a short distance until they reach easier pedaling again or leave their bikes at Mineral Park and walk. Windy Ridge appears after almost 6 miles of riding. The reward for tackling the final short climb/push is a stunning view and the chance to walk among gnarled bristlecone pines. Climb a little farther up the road to get even better views to the north (look carefully and you'll see Keystone Ski Area). The road continues winding up Mt. Bross and Mt. Lincoln; advanced riders might enjoy tackling this steep ascent.

From Windy Ridge, retrace your route to Buckskin Gulch Road. Turn left and descend for a little over a mile. Turn right onto a spur just above a small, current mining operation and across from the historic marker "B." This road crosses Buckskin Creek and heads in the direction of Buckskin Joe Mine.

Switchback left at an intersection and pass by some tailings from this sprawling mine. The road continues switchbacking up the hillside and swings around the flank of Loveland Mountain and onto the Mosquito Gulch side of the ridge. It levels out and continues climbing gradually to the west until it reaches a four-way intersection at about 12 miles. Take the left fork, which switchbacks down into the trees. You pedal through tunnels of aspen, over a creek, and down a couple of rocky switchbacks.

At the bottom of the descent you merge with another road, actually the old railroad grade, at a little over 13 miles. Turn right, ford a creek, and pass the Orphan Boy Mine that looms overhead on the right. Climb a little bit, curve to the left, and drop to a four-way intersection. Continue straight at this junction and descend farther, passing a couple of houses. You connect with County Road 12 at almost 14 miles. Turn left and follow this road through still-inhabited Park City. Beyond this small community fork left again onto County Road 10.

Follow County Road 10 another 2 miles or so into Alma. After climbing a steep hill, look to your right for a few nondescript graves that mark Park City's cemetery. With graves identified mainly by wooden crosses, this graveyard is quite a contrast to the more elaborate gravestones of Buckskin Cemetery. Climb a short distance farther and then descend into Alma. Turn left on the dirt road right before the highway and left again on County Road 8, riding back to your vehicle.

History

Buckskin Joe Mine was established early in the Colorado mining rush, during August 1859. It was named after Joe Higganbottom (he always wore deerskin clothes), the leader of a group of prospectors who discovered gold along Buckskin Creek. Although most of the mining near Buckskin was placer, several lodes were found in the area. The most famous was the Phillips lode, now called Buckskin Joe Mine, which attracted many miners

ALMA LOOP

Ride 11

to the little settlement whose population swelled to over 1,000 residents. Horace and Augusta Tabor (these were pre–Baby Doe days) ran the general store. For a while this booming community was the county seat, but it fell into decline when most of the mines played out in the late 1860s. Today not much remains; however, some of the ruins were moved to the restored mining town of South Park City near Fairplay.

The enormous Paris Mill, built in 1894, processed ore from the Paris Mine, which was discovered in 1878. The ore was transported via aerial tram from the mine high on the jagged rocks down a 750-foot vertical drop to the mill.

Park City was originally a stage and overnight stop for travelers on their way to Leadville via Mosquito Pass. After the railroad was installed, it became a stop for trains headed for the London Mines. Park City was never a large town, its population peaking at around 300 residents. The nearby Orphan Boy Mine became one of the top producers of gold around Park City and operated from the early 1860s on into the 1930s.

Comments

There is a campground up Buckskin Gulch Road, so expect some vehicles on this part. The rest of the route sees very little traffic. You pass by a lot of private property; some is marked, some isn't. Stay on the described route and away from any mining structures and workings. Some of the road numbers were being changed during 1990 and may no longer correspond with those in the description.

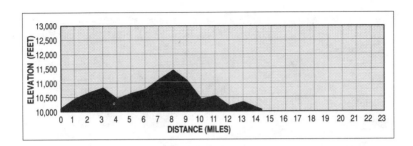

SACRAMENTO

12

Location: About 8 miles southwest of Fairplay
Distance: 14.3 miles
Time: 4 hours
Rating: Moderate–more difficult
Low Elevation: 10,100 feet
High Point: 11,440 feet
Elevation Gain: 1,340 feet
Type: Loop; dirt road, single track
Season: June–October

Maps
Trails Illustrated: Leadville/
  Fairplay South
USFS: Pike
USGS County Series: Park 1
USGS 7.5 Series: Fairplay W.

• • •

This meandering loop travels to the hillside townsite of Sacramento. A roundabout route, it explores remote ridges, follows an old wagon road, and borders the lush Fourmile Creek drainage.

Access

From Fairplay, take Hwy. 285 southwest for 3.4 miles. Turn right onto County Road 20 and drive 1.8 miles. Bear right onto a faint dirt road marked by a small orange post. You've missed it if you reach the Warm Springs Ranch gate. Follow the dirt road almost 2 miles. Go through the gate (be sure to close it) and park at the junction of FS Roads 176 and 179.

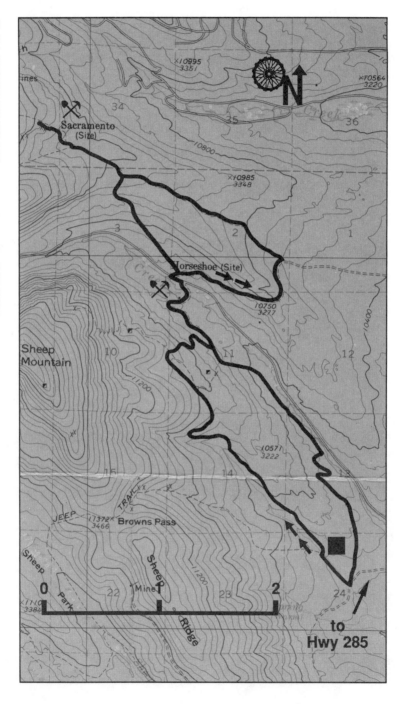

Description

Ride up the right fork, following FS Road 179 along the edge of meadows surrounding High Creek. Pass a couple faint spurs on the right and wind in and out of dense aspen groves. After about 1.5 miles a crumbling cabin appears on the right. Just beyond the cabin the road switchbacks left and then climbs left more steeply over some loose rock to a major three-way junction. Take a sharp right onto FS Road 178. Climb steeply for a short bit farther. The road then levels out and snakes along a ridge. You pass below Sheep Mountain, which looms to the west.

At an open area on the northern end of the ridge there's another three-way intersection. Take the road that swings sharply to the right (the other fork dead ends at the base of Sheep Mountain). The route, now marked by orange diamonds, begins to descend. Several steep, rocky sections test your technical skills. Continue following the orange markers, switchbacking left where a side road forks right. Descend to a four-way intersection, which you'll return to later. Go straight here and follow the road as it drops into a small meadow and swings left. Where the road heads steeply down through the trees, look for a single track on the left. Get on the single track and pedal a short distance until the track drops into the Horseshoe Campground at about 3.5 miles.

Turn right and follow the campground road out to Fourmile Road. Turn left onto this well-traveled road and follow it a short distance to a historic marker. It identifies site four, at one time the location of Horseshoe, which is hard to believe from the empty meadow that marks the area today. FS Road 18.2B forks right directly across from here. Turn right and follow what was once a wagon road as it switchbacks right and up an aspen-covered hillside. The gradual gradient makes occasional rocky sections easy to negotiate. Crest a ridge and descend to a three-way intersection at almost 5.5 miles. An interpretive sign here details the wagon road's history.

Turn left onto FS Road 18.2B and begin to climb toward Sacramento. If you love rocks, this section will be right up your alley. Gentle grades and occasional smooth sections make this otherwise rough road bearable. At about 7.5 miles you reach a meadow where the road splits. Follow the right fork as it climbs into the trees and switchbacks left. Remaining buildings of the secluded town of Sacramento appear on the right. There are actually quite a few cabins still partially standing. The mine, just a short distance farther up the road, is dominated by huge tailings piles. The road continues to climb to a knoll, but this is a much better hike than bike ride.

When returning use the junction in the meadow as a distance gauge to aid you in spotting a single track. Backtrack a little less than 0.5 miles down from the junction over one rough section of road and onto a smoother section. Look for a small open area on the right littered with rocks. There may be a *cairn* to help identify the beginning of the trail, which forks right off the road here. Turn into this open area and look for a single track that curves right into the trees just beyond the rocks. It doesn't get much use and is faint at first. This trail drops southwest for a very short distance, curves to the right, and passes a mining pit on the left. Just beyond the pit you'll need to walk your bike over an extremely rocky section that also has some fallen timber. This area is marked by a large field of rock to the left. The trail swings left after this and continues south along the ridge for a short distance. It then drops steeply, sometimes over challenging sections of loose rock, and continues through trees and into the Fourmile drainage.

Eventually leveling out a little, the trail travels south until coming back out at a little over 9 miles at the junction of Fourmile Road and the wagon road you were on earlier. Turn left onto Fourmile Road, retracing your route to the campground and back onto the single track identified by a wood post on the left. Backtrack a bit farther, ride through the meadow, turn right, and then climb briefly to the four-way intersection you crossed earlier.

This time take the left fork, which is also marked by orange diamonds. A continuation of the same historic wagon road, the fork heads south, descends along the right side of Fourmile Creek, and travels through a meadow along the edge of the trees. It merges with a road from the left, passes a spur that climbs to the right, and crosses a small bog where the route becomes faint. It's easy to pick up again and is well marked by the orange markers.

Around 11.5 miles, the road curves sharply and steeply up to the right. It climbs through a series of short, steep ascents onto a ridge. Then meandering becomes the norm as you ride along the ridge in a southwesterly direction. Side roads appear now and then, and the orange markers eventually fork off onto one of these, but the main route remains the most obvious. It finally drops onto a road in the drainage where your vehicle is parked. From the junction near a "Road Closed" sign, turn right and pedal the short distance back to your vehicle.

History

For much of this ride you follow what was once a heavily traveled wagon road. Originating in Fairplay, the road was a major artery that linked mines up the various drainages and went all the way to the Weston Pass Road. It provided access to Sacramento and its nearby mines and eventually connected down to Horseshoe, beyond to Mullenville (where Warm Springs Ranch is today), and then on to the pass road.

Horseshoe, named after the impressive horseshoe-shaped mountain just up the drainage, was near the sites of early silver strikes in the valley.

The only easily visible remnant of this camp is the slag pile left over from the smelter that operated here. It's located southwest of the road just beyond the historic marker. Incorporated in 1881, Horseshoe had a population of about 300 and in addition to being a mining and lumbering center was a stop for a spur of the railroad that served mines farther up the valley. The camp was deserted by 1907, and vandals later began destroying the buildings.

Sacramento developed after several claims were located in the area by men returning from silver fields in distant mountains. The Sacramento Mining Company was formed in 1878. After ore from this region was displayed in Fairplay, miners flocked to the hillside, necessitating a boarding house, cabins, and the other buildings that create a community. More profitable mines opened, with the most activity generated during 1881–1882. Never a large community, Sacramento supported a peak population of about 100 residents. Inaccessibility and average-grade ore spelled the doom of the short-lived settlement.

Comments

It takes sharp eyes to spot, and at first to follow, the single track, but the trail becomes more obvious after about 0.5 miles of riding. Beautiful aspen groves make fall a good time to try this ride. Much of the area in and around Sacramento is privately owned. Please respect it as such. During 1990, the Forest Service was renumbering roads and replacing orange route markers with blue ones. Expect some differences between the written description and the markings you actually see.

Few cabins still stand in the Sacramento townsite.

Ride 13 · Leadville Loop

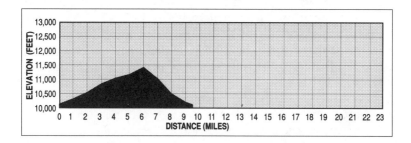

LEADVILLE LOOP

13

Location: Leadville
Distance: 9.5 miles
Time: 2–3 hours
Rating: Easy*–moderate
Low Elevation: 10,150 feet
High Point: 11,440 feet
Elevation Gain: 1,290 feet
Type: Loop; dirt road, pavement
Season: June–early October

This route follows a well-maintained dirt road and contains only one very short, steep section that is rideable, although a novice may choose to walk it.

Maps
Trails Illustrated: Breckenridge South, Leadville/Fairplay South
USFS: San Isabel
USGS County Series: Lake
USGS 7.5 Series: Leadville N., Leadville S., Climax, Mt. Sherman

• • •

The "Route of the Silver Kings" climbs above the east side of Leadville through much of its historic mining district. Mt. Elbert, Colorado's highest peak, provides a striking backdrop to the numerous mining remains that make this an outdoor museum.

Access

From the main street of Leadville (Harrison Avenue) turn east onto an alley (marked by a sign for "Free RV Parking") between the Tabor Opera House and KG Food Store. Park in the lot behind the opera house.

Description

Pedal out to Harrison Avenue. Turn right and ride a few blocks to 7th Street. Hang a right on 7th Street and begin to climb out of town. Upon reaching the outskirts of Leadville you become immersed in the tailings of Fryer Hill. Rising majestically out of the trees above you on the right, just before the Matchless Mine, is the headframe of the Wright shaft. Shortly after, on the left, is the entrance to the Matchless Mine. There's an entry fee but if you don't feel like paying just peek through the fence to catch a glimpse of the cabin where Baby Doe Tabor froze to death while waiting to regain her fame and fortune. At about 1.7 miles the route changes from pavement to a well-maintained dirt road and climbs gradually toward an imposing mountain cirque. You'll notice a lot of side roads in this area. They are all on private property and it is imperative that you stay on the designated route.

At almost 3 miles you approach a major junction where the town of Evansville once sat. Continue left on the main road. It passes the Famous Mine on the left and runs below the Fortune Mine, located across the valley on the right. As Evans Gulch begins to open up, the enormous impact mining had on this area becomes apparent. Even after one hundred years some hillsides remain denuded of trees. After about 4.3 miles of riding you see a road that forks to the left near a current mining operation. This is the beginning of Mosquito Pass Road, the old stage route over the Mosquito Range to Fairplay and now a popular mountain bike ride. Stay on the main road, which curves to the right and heads back to the west. An overwhelming view of a great wall of mountains dominated by Mt. Elbert rises above shimmering Turquoise Lake.

The road becomes slightly rougher as it climbs a hill, giving you a close-up view of the Fortune Mine. Curve around the hill to the left and drop into South Evans Gulch. Pass a well-traveled road that switchbacks right and descends past the remaining buildings of Stumptown, which lie in the open areas of this gulch. Continue on the route that travels up the drainage. Once again there are several side roads. Ride under some powerlines and cross a small creek. After you tackle the only steep, rough (but short) section of this ride, curve to the right for a much more gradual climb up another hill. The road follows a railroad grade for a short distance and passes several more mines including the enormous Fanny Rawlins, which, defying age and decay, remains standing.

You merge with another main dirt road at roughly 6.5 miles. Turn right and follow the road on a long descent into Leadville. It's easy to get carried away on this fun downhill, but there's still plenty to look at so a leisurely pace is recommended. After riding through some trees you break out into a small meadow where the town of Adelaide sat. Just before the edge of town the road passes between the enormous Robert Emmett Mine and the collapsed remains of Finntown. The road changes to pavement and takes you back onto Harrison Avenue near your vehicle.

History

Leadville was one of the dominating producers of minerals in Colorado and the majority of its mining was located on the hills east of town. Although gold was discovered, it was silver that made Leadville famous and many men wealthy. There is a lot to see and not enough room to write about all of it, so only the major settlements and mines are described.

The first silver discovery of significance was made by George Fryer on what is now known as Fryer Hill, on the edge of town up 7th Street. East of Fryer Hill the slopes are cluttered with many old mine workings, dumps, and remains of settlements. One of the more visible sites is the Wright shaft, with its massive headframe still intact, perched above a 320-foot shaft. Called a Cornish headframe, this structure is typical of the type used in mines in Cornwall, England.

The Matchless Mine, one of the more famous due to its owners, Horace and Baby Doe Tabor, was bought for $117,000 and for quite some time received monthly returns of $100,000. It is the site where Baby Doe froze to death, determined to hold on to the mine and make it profitable again after Horace, on his deathbed, pleaded, "Hold on to the Matchless." For a while Horace and Baby Doe were one of the richest and most flamboyant couples of Colorado's mining era, but the silver crash of 1893 destroyed them and Baby Doe spent her last years living alone in this cabin.

Stumptown, almost a Leadville suburb, was a large residential community in south Evans Gulch. The town developed around the many mines in the area, with about 20 homes, a few saloons, and an extremely popular pool hall. It was abandoned in the 1930s, but there are many remaining houses in various states of disrepair along the creek. Another settlement east of Leadville, Adelaide, grew up around the Adelaide Mine, one of the earliest and richest mines in this gulch. With discovery of more and more mines in the area Adelaide prospered and gained a reputation as a wild community with lots of gambling and fighting. Nothing remains in the pretty little meadow that once held at least 36 cabins and 28 businesses. Down the road are the few remaining buildings of Finntown. During its heyday, this area was almost one continuous town from Leadville to Adelaide. Originally home to a colony of immigrants from England, it was eventually inhabited by Finns and Swedes. The Robert Emmett Mine, across the road, was the site of violent labor disputes between the miners and mine guards during the intense strikes of 1896.

Comments

Although this ride is appropriate for novices, keep in mind that elevations here are high, always above 10,000 feet. The hillsides east of Leadville are riddled with deep shafts and underground tunnels. It is critical to stay on the described route, never venturing off the main roadways. You would be trespassing and putting yourself in danger. There are current mining operations up both these roads, so there may be truck traffic. Late afternoon is a good time to ride, as well as weekends. "The Route of the Silver Kings," a brochure for sale at the Chamber of Commerce, describes in detail the area east of Leadville if you're interested in additional information.

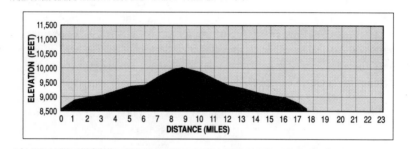

CHALK CREEK

14

Although this ride changes to a moderate rating after Alpine, novices can continue to St. Elmo by following the described ride option.

Location: About 13 miles southwest of Buena Vista
Distance: 17.5 miles
Time: 3–4 hours
Rating: Easy*–moderate
Low Elevation: 8,560 feet
High Point: 10,000 feet
Elevation Gain: 1,440 feet
Type: Out and back, loop; dirt road
Season: Late May–October

Maps
Trails Illustrated: Shavano Peak
USFS: San Isabel
USGS County Series: Chaffee 2
USGS 7.5 Series: St. Elmo, Mt. Antero

• • •

Ride **14**   CHALK CREEK

CHALK CREEK

Ride 14

Much of this route follows the old South Park and Pacific Railroad grade that crossed through the heart of the Collegiate Mountains. This ride passes magnificent white granite cliffs below Mt. Princeton, small roadside lakes, and soaring peaks before ending among the quaint buildings that line St. Elmo's main street.

Access

From Buena Vista drive 7.5 miles south on Hwy. 285. Turn right onto County Road 162 at the sign for Mt. Princeton Hot Springs and St. Elmo. Drive 5.4 miles and turn left onto County Road 290. Follow this dirt road until it dead ends. Park in the large turn-around.

Description

Begin pedaling up the railroad grade. Actually a continuation of the county road, the grade is blocked off to motor vehicles. From this route high above the valley you get an excellent view of the crevices and caves within the Chalk Cliffs. It is rumored that a couple of bags of precious treasure, taken by Spaniards from an Indian camp, lie hidden among the cliffs. You follow a shelf road that was carved into the mountainside to accommodate the narrow-gauge train. The nearly level grade makes pedaling a breeze. A couple of rock slides have deposited debris on the road but it's easy to get around. There is one creek crossing you may need to wade, depending on its level and your stream-crossing ability.

After about 2 miles the grade merges with the main dirt road that climbs up the valley. Continue up this road for about a mile. There may be some traffic but the short duration of time you're on the road and the beauty of the surroundings make it tolerable. Cross a new-looking bridge and turn left onto Road 292. Follow this less-traveled route, originally a wagon road to Alpine, as it climbs along the right side of Chalk Creek. You pass several beaver ponds and ride through thick canopies of aspen. There are some spur roads, most leading to summer cottages, along the next few miles of pedaling. The main route remains easy to follow.

After roughly 5.3 miles you reach a three-way junction at Alpine Lake. The early community of Alpine sat in this area but now summer cabins cover the site. The described route, which changes to a moderate rating here, follows the right fork. Beginners who want a continuation of smooth, gradual riding can turn left and pedal a short distance until they reach the main road. Turn right onto this road and follow it to St. Elmo. Expect traffic on this optional route. To follow the described ride, curve around the right side of Alpine Lake. Just beyond it the road becomes rougher and begins the first of several short, moderate climbs. You ascend high above a steep, narrow canyon carved by Chalk Creek.

After you drop back down by some beaver ponds the terrain becomes easy again. Watch for the only remaining structure of Iron City (its power plant), tucked back into the trees along the right side of the road. An interpretive sign on the side of the building details its history. Just beyond Iron City look for the St. Elmo Cemetery concealed in the trees on the right. The road then passes by a campground, crosses the creek, and merges with the main road. Turn right and pedal a short distance farther onto the picturesque main street of St. Elmo. If you're looking for a place for a lunch break, ride through town and follow either Road 267 or 294. They both offer plenty of places to stop and rest. For your trip back you have a choice. You can either return as you came or follow the main road, which descends along the other side of Chalk Creek. If you choose the second option you will have some traffic to deal with. I returned along this route. It was late in the afternoon and the road wasn't busy. The smooth route surface made it a fun, fast cruise. Be sure to fork right onto the less used section of grade at the end of the ride, which takes you back to your vehicle.

History

Alpine was incorporated in 1879 and quickly reached a peak population of about 500 people by 1880. It was mainly a supply town for other camps farther up the valley and also had an ore processing mill. Quite a variety of buildings were constructed including a dance hall, two hotels, three banks, and as many as 23 saloons. Once the railroad moved farther up the valley Alpine's population began to dwindle. Many residents moved to St. Elmo, often taking their houses and stores with them!

Iron City was known for its smelter and power plant. For a while this smelter treated most of the ore in the district, but once the train came and was able to ship ore out, the smelter was no longer needed. The power plant was part of an ambitious project. Its electricity, sent an amazing distance via powerlines over Tincup Pass, was used by a dredge operating in a gulch below Tincup. Iron City was also deserted once new towns were established farther up the valley. A collapse of a dam on a nearby reservoir washed away most of Iron City's buildings.

Originally named Forest City because of surrounding groves of trees, St. Elmo was laid out in 1879. The town acquired its current name the next year. St. Elmo was always a major transportation hub. At first it accommodated freight wagons and stages, which left town daily for Tincup, Aspen, and settlements to the south. The community was also the jumping-off point for miners who worked nearby goldfields. By 1881 the town had railroad service. Mining, railroading, and stage transportation industries kept St. Elmo operating at a frantic pace. It remained the largest town in the district even after the railroad continued farther up the valley. In addition, St. Elmo was a lively "Saturday night town." Men from the upper mining camps and crews working on the train tunnel created a boisterous atmosphere. Between 1,500 and 2,000 people lived in St. Elmo during 1882. Closure of the railroad in 1926 and the opening of a shorter freight route to Aspen via Independence Pass marked the beginning of St. Elmo's decline.

Comments

Expect some traffic if you choose to ride any sections of the main road. A few people still live in St. Elmo and "No Trespassing" signs are common. Please respect any private property in this area. Numerous aspen groves make fall riding in this drainage a treat.

St. Elmo, with its well-preserved main street, is the destination of the Chalk Creek ride.

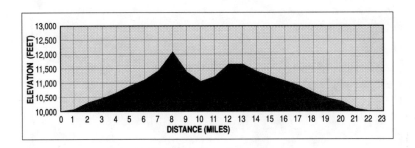

ALPINE TUNNEL

15

*The first few miles up the railroad grade are easy pedaling. Once the turnoff for Hancock Pass is reached, the rating changes to advanced.

Location: About 23 miles south-west of Buena Vista
Distance: 22 miles
Time: 5–6 hours
Rating: Easy*–advanced
Low Elevation: 10,000 feet
High Point: 12,080 feet
Elevation Gain: 2,080 feet
Type: Out and back, loop; dirt road
Season: Late June–September

Maps
Trails Illustrated: Shavano Peak
USFS: San Isabel, Gunnison
USGS County Series: Chaffee 2, 3, Gunnison 5
USGS 7.5 Series: St. Elmo, Whitepine, Cumberland Pass, Hancock

• • •

The Alpine Tunnel, one of Colorado's great railroad engineering feats, is the destination of this ride. Additional highlights of this superb backcountry tour include riding deep into the Collegiate Mountains and crossing a spectacular high alpine pass.

Access

From Buena Vista, drive 7.5 miles south on Hwy. 285. Turn right onto County Road 162 at the sign for Mt. Princeton Hot Springs and St. Elmo. Follow this road for 15.3 miles as it climbs along Chalk Creek and turns

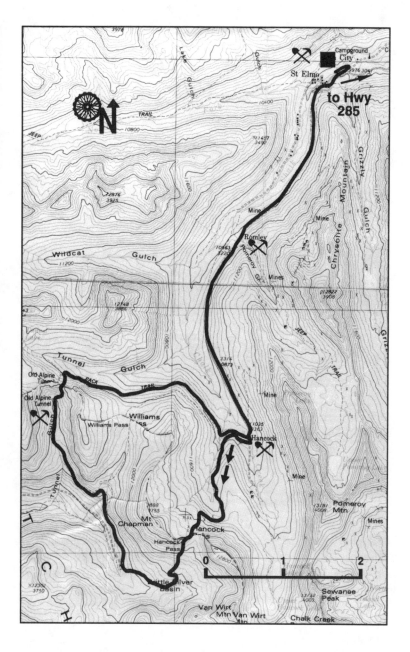

to dirt before reaching St. Elmo. Park in a large pullout on the right of the road just before the town.

Description

Ride back down the main road a short distance and take a sharp right onto County Road 295 toward Hancock. The road climbs gradually over easy terrain along the hillside railroad grade. Mines and other old buildings appear periodically above and below the road all the way to Hancock. Some are obvious; others are tucked in the trees. Take your time and be observant.

After crossing a bridge at about 3 miles you pass mining debris and collapsed buildings on the right that mark the Romley townsite. More well-preserved structures appear at almost 5 miles, including an enormous ore bin that perches precariously over the road. Ride out of the trees and into the upper valley, passing the few remains of Hancock on the left. After crossing a bridge you encounter a three-way junction near a trailhead parking area. Turn left onto FS Road 295.2 and follow the road toward Hancock Lake/Hancock Pass. At this point the ride rating changes to advanced. The road gets a lot rougher and soon steep climbs begin.

Shortly after the first junction take a sharp right toward Hancock Pass at a second junction. The road gets a lot rockier as it winds in and out of stands of pine and willow-filled meadows until it climbs above timberline. Wildflowers take over where trees left off, covering many hillsides. Completely rideable but challenging both physically and technically, the road climbs to the exposed saddle of Hancock Pass at about 8 miles. If the weather is good you can relax at the top and soak up the views.

Sheer walls in Brittle Silver Basin provide a dramatic backdrop for your descent down the other side of Hancock Pass. You drop steeply through tundra-covered hillsides for about a mile to a three-way junction. Turn right onto FS Road 888. Cross a creek and continue to descend over a rock-filled section of road until you reach a major three-way intersection at roughly 9.7 miles. Turn right onto the railroad grade, which takes you up to the Alpine Tunnel. Interpretive signs that detail interesting features of this grade appear periodically along the road.

After the workout of Hancock Pass you'll appreciate the easy pedaling of this well-maintained grade. A quick glance at the jagged cliffs above and below the road is sure to generate amazement at the location of a railroad grade on a seemingly impenetrable mountainside. After about 12 miles of pedaling you round a corner and ride beyond a gate and past rubble from the structures built near the western portal of the tunnel. A few buildings remain, including the old station, which has some fascinating literature posted inside on the walls. It's worth it to spend some time poking around,

ALPINE TUNNEL

piecing together the history of the railroad and gaining appreciation of the effort that was put into this project.

Follow the grade up to the now collapsed tunnel entrance. Take the trail that branches off to the right of the tunnel and climbs to a saddle above it. You may have to walk part of this. A thrilling single-track descent brings you near the also collapsed eastern portal of the tunnel. Turn left to inspect the other entrance and right to complete the loop. This side of the grade sees less traffic, and quite a few ties remain on the road. It's rideable but be prepared for a jarring descent. You circle back to the trailhead parking and the beginning of Hancock Pass Road at approximately 16 miles. From here return the way you came following the lower part of the grade back to your vehicle.

History

Ride 15

St. Elmo, your starting place, has been beautifully preserved and even supports a few residents. When incorporated in 1880, it had only 400 inhabitants but eventually grew to a population of 1,500–3,000 people. In addition to being near mining, the town was an important transportation hub, the starting point for a stage line that operated over Tincup Pass as well as for toll roads to Aspen and the south. St. Elmo was a popular "Saturday night town" and become exceptionally lively when workers constructing the railroad paid their visits.

Romley grew up around the successful Mary Murphy Mine. Located up the slope from the town, this mine employed hundreds of men. It became the largest producer in the district and had both valuable gold and silver ore. Established in the 1870s, Romley survived until the nearby mines played out. Closure of the railroad in 1926 caused its ultimate death. Though the only remains are in the meadow below the road, Romley sprawled down the hillside and into the trees.

An important railroad town, Hancock was the end of the line until the Alpine Tunnel was built. It then became an important stop for the train and provided housing for the workers who labored to keep the treacherous stretch of grade from Hancock to the tunnel open. Also a mining town, it was established originally around some claims, but the prospecting was short-lived.

A decision was made by the Denver, South Park, and Pacific Railroad in 1879 to bore a tunnel through the Continental Divide, achieving a shorter, faster route into the Gunnison Valley. Work began on the Alpine Tunnel project in 1880. Estimated to take half a year, tunneling actually consumed 23 months. About 450 men worked on the project at a given time but the strenuous labor caused a high turnover rate. The tunnel was first used in December 1881. For the time and money put into this endeavor—around

$242 thousand — it remained open a very short time, closing in 1910. This incredible engineering accomplishment used 400,000 feet of redwood timber to shore the walls and ceiling and contained 1,771 feet of track. It was the first tunnel to carry tracks under the Continental Divide and at the time was the highest point reached by a railroad. Collapsed timbers at the entrance of each portal are the remains of protective snowsheds. On the western side only the restored station remains standing. Next to it are timbers of a collapsed boarding house and across the grade is the stone foundation of the engine house, which could store up to six engines.

Comments

This ride works well for a group with varying skill levels. Novices will enjoy the first few miles of pedaling up the gradual, well-maintained railroad grade. While experienced riders tackle the advanced section of the ride, those who stay behind can explore the high alpine valleys around Hancock and the eastern portal of the Alpine Tunnel. Choose a good-weather day for this ride and get an early start. You spend a lot of time above timberline, where a thunderstorm can be dangerous. Please be conscientious about signs and structures along this route. A lot of effort has been put into preserving the Alpine Tunnel's history.

ADDITIONAL RIDES IN REGION 2

• • •

Gold Hill

This moderate–more difficult loop, excellent for perfecting single-track skills, climbs and descends over forested terrain near Frisco. The trail starts from a parking area 4.6 miles south of Frisco on Hwy. 9. The first 4 miles climb over sometimes rocky terrain and through several logged-out areas. Then the real fun begins with a descent to a trail junction. Turn right onto the Peaks Trail for more downhill until the trail merges with Miner's Creek Road. Follow this road down to the paved bikepath. Turn right onto the bikepath, pedal a few more miles, and you're back at your vehicle. The majority of this 12-mile route is marked by blue diamonds attached to trees, making navigation a bit easier.

North, Middle, and South Forks of the Swan

Each of these three roads takes you up a separate drainage of the Swan River. Ghost towns and mining remains combined with creekside pedaling up to timberline views make each route a great mountain-bike ride. Out and back rides, they all travel about 5 miles to a destination. The South Fork climbs to Georgia Pass; the Middle and North Forks pass old mining settlements and ascend to high alpine cirques. Accessed up Tiger Road (near the Breckenridge Golf Course), these rides start out with a few miles of easy pedaling and then change to more difficult ratings as the routes get steeper. Many side roads and trails offer even more biking possibilities.

Beaver Ridge

The variety of terrain around Beaver Ridge accommodates a wide range of bikers. The first few miles along FS Road 659, accessed beyond the Fairplay Nordic Center, offer easy pedaling along Beaver Creek. Intermediate and advanced bikers can pedal either 9-mile or 11-mile loops that climb over the ridge, drop into the meadows of High Park, and circle back via county roads. There's also a road forking off the longer loop that climbs toward the top of Mt. Silverheels. The open meadows along Beaver Creek, windswept ridgetops supporting bristlecone pines, and cool groves of aspen provide a variety of scenery.

Crooked Creek–Trout Creek

Winding through some of the most expansive aspen groves I've ever seen, the Crooked Creek–Trout Creek Forest Service roads offer superb mountain-bike terrain for novice through advanced riders. Crooked Creek Road starts from Silverheels Ranch County Road, which is accessed just northeast of Fairplay near the ballpark. This 12.5-mile, out and back route follows FS Roads 669 and 194 through smooth, rolling terrain, easy stream crossings, and dense aspen groves for the first few miles. After you cross Trout Creek, the terrain becomes more technically challenging. The road climbs along the creek to a good turn-around point near some old cabins at the base of Mt. Silverheels. Winter trails, identified by orange markers, spur off the main route and offer additional opportunities for exploring. A small logging operation has altered the road and done some clearing but this doesn't negatively affect the fun of riding in this area.

Bear Gulch–Long Park Loop

Well worth the drive from Fairplay, this beautiful 10.5-mile loop explores the foothills around Buffalo Peaks. Contrasts in scenery range from lush hillside stands of aspen to wide open meadows in Long Park. Access this ride by driving 12.4 miles southwest of Fairplay on Hwy. 285. Then follow Buffalo Peaks Road for about 3 miles and park at a three-way junction near the edge of Long Park and FS Road 432. Pedal up Buffalo Peaks Road for another 3 miles, and then turn right onto Bear Gulch FS Road 158. Minimal climbing and a wonderful descent bring you to Rough and Tumbling Creek, which you ford and descend along for roughly 1.3 miles. After you turn right onto a road that crosses the creek again, ride into Long Park, fork right onto FS Road 432, and loop back to your vehicle. Although gradual climbs and smooth roads make this easy riding, any biker would enjoy this scenic cruise.

Mitchell Creek

This 8-mile loop covers a variety of terrain including the Colorado Trail, a navigationally challenging descent along Mitchell Creek, and an easy ascent along a railroad grade. A moderate ride, it originates north of Leadville on Tennessee Pass. From the trailhead near the restrooms on the pass, follow a single track for about 2.7 miles. Where the trail crosses a main dirt road, fork right and climb up this road until you reach Wurts Ditch. Cross over the ditch and look for blue diamonds marking a cross-country ski route that takes off from the right side of the road and into the trees. For the next 1.7 miles you follow these blue diamonds off and on as well as an overgrown road as you descend along the right side of Mitchell Creek drainage. This section is navigationally challenging. At the bottom of the drainage you merge with a dirt road that climbs back to Tennessee Pass along an old railroad grade.

Mt. Champion

The road to Mt. Champion climbs through a lush high alpine meadow containing a beautiful old mill and several other mining structures. Massive peaks line both sides of this route. The ride originates at the Elbert Creek Campground on Halfmoon Creek Road, which is accessed about 4.5 miles southwest of Leadville. The first 3 miles consist of moderate pedaling as the road climbs along Halfmoon Creek. Beyond a small cabin a longer, more difficult climb brings you into the peak-rimmed valley that contains the mill. After pedaling for about 5.5 miles you reach a gate near the head of the valley. Public access ends here, but you'll be able to get a good view of Champion Mill and the surrounding buildings.

Colorado Trail

Between Leadville and Monarch Pass the Colorado Trail offers several sections of superb biking. One route goes from Halfmoon Creek Road (accessed just southwest of Leadville) to Twin Lakes. To avoid an initially steep climb from the Mt. Elbert trailhead, use the lower Forest Service roads that fork left about 1 mile up Halfmoon Creek Road. A quick look at the Trails Illustrated maps for this area shows you how to follow Lodgepole Flats Road until it merges with the Colorado Trail just beyond Mill Creek. The trail contours along the base of Mt. Elbert for about 3 miles, crossing through small drainages and around small ponds. It eventually drops to a parking area above Twin Lakes.

To loop back follow County Road 24 around Forebay Reservoir and down to a dirt road that heads north. A left turn onto Sage Draw Road takes you back up to Lodgepole Flats Road, where you fork right to return to your vehicle. This 16.5-mile moderate loop has some spectacular trail riding. Another moderate, extremely rideable section of the Colorado Trail travels from Bald Mountain (near Buena Vista) to Mt. Princeton Hot Springs. Although best done with a shuttle vehicle left at the hot springs, this ride can also be done as an out and back. Gain most of the elevation in a vehicle by driving up Bald Mountain (County Road 345) and parking at the last switchback before the radio tower. Follow the old road that forks west from this switchback. When it ends you bushwhack a short distance to find the trail. Then it's great single-track cruising for approximately 5 miles until the trail merges with Mt. Princeton Road. Descend along this road if you have a shuttle waiting at the hot springs or turn around and return to Bald Mountain.

South Fork of Lake Creek

This road provides easy access into high country valleys filled with wildflowers, tumbling creeks, and rugged mountains. From Leadville, take Hwy. 24 south and turn right onto Hwy. 82 toward Independence

Pass. Drive 14 miles to the South Fork Road. Park and pedal up a short, moderate grade until the trail opens into a classic high alpine valley containing easy riding. A choice of three different drainages to pedal up, with round-trip distances ranging from 8–12 miles, means you can spend a few hours or a whole day exploring this region. Sayre Gulch is the least traveled, the South Fork of Lake Creek drainage is carpeted with columbines in midsummer, and Peekaboo Gulch offers intermediate climbing. All routes end at wilderness area boundaries. Truly spectacular scenery enhances this enjoyable ride.

Fourmile

A number of loop possibilities exist off of Fourmile Road, which climbs into the foothills east of Buena Vista. Full of beautiful rock outcrops, this unique terrain is frequently ridden year-round due to a lower elevation and drier climate. To reach Fourmile Road from Buena Vista follow County Road 371 across the Arkansas River to a junction where Fourmile Road (#375) forks right. A moderate 11-mile ride starts at the junction of FS Roads 375 and 376.1. Pedal over the rolling terrain of Road 376.1 until you fork left onto 311.1. Using this road plus FS Roads 311.A, 373, and 375. A, you make a large loop that climbs in and out of several small drainages, along the base of a spectacular cliff, and through ponderosa pine forests. You eventually ride back onto Fourmile Road, which you follow down to your vehicle.

Turret

Starting on high aspen ridges east of the Arkansas River, the road to the ghost town of Turret drops into desert-like foothills that contain beautiful rock formations. A long drive to the trailhead follows Hwy. 285 east from Buena Vista and then takes county and Forest Service roads south for another 11 miles to Aspen Ridge. But it's worth it because you see very few people, although this moderate 20-mile ride follows well-maintained roads. After the initial climb up Aspen Ridge it's downhill for 5 miles until you reach a road that forks right. This road climbs to a high point with great views of the Collegiate Range before it descends another 2 miles into the gulch where well-preserved remains of Turret dot the hillsides. You return along the same route, which means a lot of climbing, but a smooth road surface and fairly moderate grades make the ascent tolerable.

Bikeable Passes

Bikeable passes in Region 2 include Webster, Georgia, French, Boreas, Wheeler, Ptarmigan, Searle, Shrine, Mosquito, Weston, Hagerman, Cottonwood, Tincup, Hancock, and Old Monarch. Many of these passes make great day trips and accommodate a wide range of skill levels.

Region 3
West Central Colorado

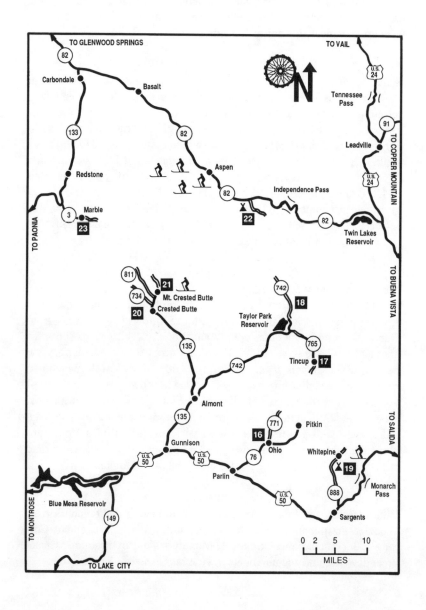

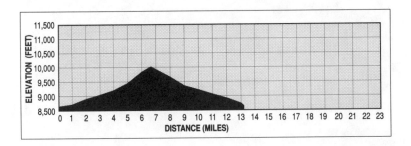

GOLD CREEK

16

Although the majority of this route is gradual and smooth, a couple of rough spots necessitate the addition of a moderate rating.

Location: About 20 miles east of Gunnison
Distance: 13.2 miles
Time: 3.5 hours
Rating: Easy*–moderate
Low Elevation: 8,640 feet
High Point: 10,000 feet
Elevation Gain: 1,360 feet
Type: Out and back; dirt road
Season: May–October

Maps
Trails Illustrated: Gunnison NE
USFS: Gunnison
USGS County Series: Gunnison 5
USGS 7.5 Series: Pitkin, Fairview Peak

• • •

This creekside ride passes several large mines as it climbs gradually through aspen groves and past dilapidated buildings to reach meadows that surround the upper Gold Creek drainage.

Access

From Gunnison drive 11 miles east on Hwy 50. Turn left at the fork for Ohio City/Quartz Creek Valley and follow paved County Road 76 for 9 miles until you reach Ohio City. You can either park on the right under the "RV Parking" sign next to the store (ask the store owner's permission first) or park across the street at the post office if it's after 11 A.M. and the office is closed.

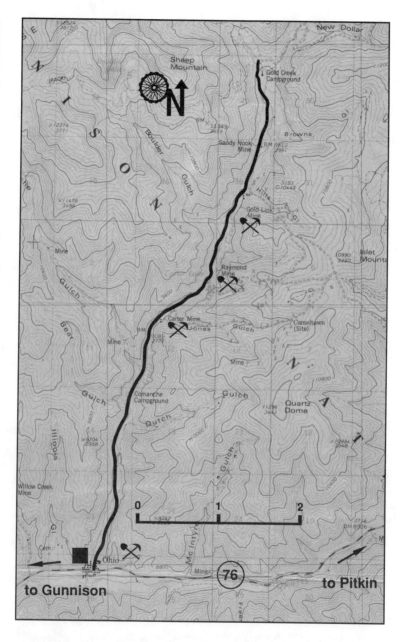

GOLD CREEK

Sheep Mountain

N

New Dollar

Gold Creek Campground

Browns

Sandy Hook Mine

Gold Link Mine

Raymond Mine

Islet Mounta

Carter Mine

Jones

Cameltown (Site)

Gulch

Mine

Mine

Comanche Campground

Gulch

Gulch

Quartz Dome

Willow Creek Mine

0   1   2

Cem

Ohio

Mine

76

to Gunnison

to Pitkin

Description

This seems like an unlikely place for any mining activity, but you'll be surprised at how many large operations are located in this drainage. To access Gold Creek pedal a short distance farther up the county road. Just after the bridge turn left onto County Road 771 at a sign for Gold Creek. This well-maintained dirt road offers extremely easy riding conditions for the first 2 miles as it passes some houses and climbs up the valley. Beyond the campground the canyon narrows and its steep walls more closely border the road. Three large mines pulled ore from the Gold Creek drainage; quite a few buildings line the creek as a result. Many of them are hidden back in the trees but can be seen if you're observant. I enjoyed the challenge of spotting these crumbling structures and saw several on the descent that I didn't notice while I pedaled up.

You pass the first mine, the Carter, after about 3 miles of pedaling. It has been worked recently and is somewhat modernized. Other than the deserted house across the road, the most impressive old feature is the wall of wood cribbing that still stands near the mine. As you continue to climb you ride over some rougher sections of road. You won't need much technical ability to deal with these spots, just the stamina to withstand some bouncing and jiggling.

The Raymond Mine appears at almost 4 miles. There's a lot of mining junk scattered on both sides of the road. You pass under an old cable that spans the drainage and ride around a large tailings pile near some impressive stonework from the mill foundation. Farther up the road are some beautifully aged buildings that have managed to remain upright. Less than a mile beyond are the Gold Link Mine and its impressive stamp mill. Quite a few original buildings sit upstream from the mine. You'll have to look carefully to see them. They're tucked into the trees beyond a fence on the right side of the road.

The road continues to climb gradually and passes a beautiful private residence on the right. After some meandering through the pines and passing the few remains of the much smaller Sandy Hook Mine on the left, you reach Gold Creek Campground. Several trails start from this area. Although generally too steep for biking, they are great hikes and might be worth exploring if you have some time. The ride ends here, but Gold Creek Road continues up the drainage. Riders with some technical skill can pedal for another 1.5 miles until the road turns to single track. It is rocky at first but eventually levels out and wanders through a small, quiet valley. I saw several nice lunch spots near sandy bars along the creek. When descending to your vehicle, keep your speed in check around blind corners on the road.

History

Gold was found around this area in the 1860s but it was the discovery of silver that sparked a rush to Ohio City and the Gold Creek drainage. By 1880 the town had close to 50 cabins and several frame buildings including stores, restaurants, and saloons. After the silver market's collapse in 1893 Ohio City was on the verge of desertion until it made a comeback with the beginning of gold mining in 1896. The area along Gold Creek became a rich gold district.

The Carter Mine actually consisted of a group of 79 patented claims. A mile-and-a-half long tunnel was used to reach veins of high value ore that had been worked in the early stages of Ohio City's mining activity. Carroll Carter spent millions of dollars on his mining operation, and its success became apparent when $3,000 worth of gold brick was shipped every two weeks during the early 1900s. Production in the Carter Mine continued until 1942. The Raymond was one of the older mines in the region and also one of the most active. A 2,700-foot tunnel was bored and produced such a high amount of ore that a $50,000 mill was built in 1905 to process it. Over $7 million of ore was produced by 1916. In 1917 the Raymond Mine shut down.

The biggest mill on the creek is the 40-stamp mill at the Gold Links Mine. The company that operated this mine held over 6,000 acres of land. A 4,000-foot tunnel ran from the creek into the mountain, cutting through many veins that produced both gold and silver ore. Although never as spectacular a producer as some of the other mines, the Gold Links was quite active from 1870 until 1915 and proved to be highly successful with its gold production.

Comments

Most of the spurs that branch off from this route lead to private property. They are well marked and are easily avoided. The signed Forest Service roads that fork off to the right might be worth exploring for riders comfortable with steep climbs. Numerous cabins and other mining structures line the drainages these roads ascend. Much of Gold Creek Road is lined with aspen and the fall riding is beautiful.

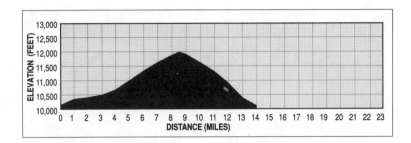

CUMBERLAND PASS LOOP

17

The grade to Cumberland Pass gains quite a bit of elevation but is gradual and can be pedaled by a novice.

Location: About 40 miles northeast of Gunnison

Distance: 14 miles

Time: 3–4 hours

Rating: Easy*–more difficult

Low Elevation: 10,160 feet

High Point: 12,000 feet

Elevation Gain: 1,840 feet

Type: Loop; dirt road

Season: Late June–early October

Maps

Trails Illustrated: Collegiate Peaks, Shavano Peak

USFS: Gunnison

USGS County Series: Gunnison 3,5

USGS 7.5 Series: Cumberland Pass, Tincup

• • •

The Cumberland Pass Road travels along willow-covered drainages, cool pine forests, and windswept slopes of tundra and talus. A descent along a side route that crosses heavily forested Duncan Hill passes many historic structures.

Access

From Gunnison drive about 11 miles north on Hwy. 135 to the junction at Almont. Take the right fork and drive about 22 miles toward Taylor Park Reservoir. Turn right onto Road 765 at the sign for Tincup. Drive for 8 miles and park on the right in the lot next to the Tincup store.

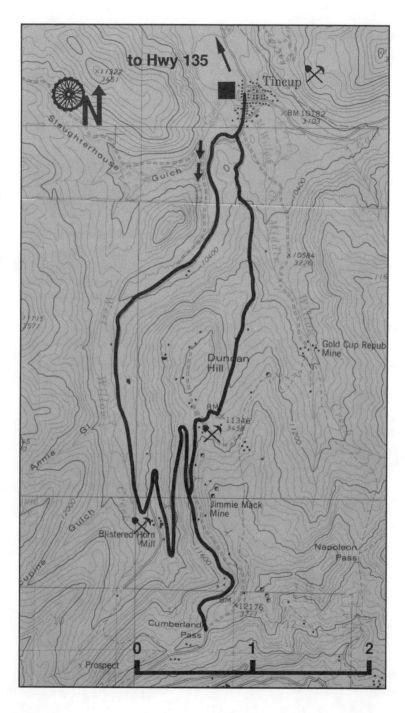

Ride 17 CUMBERLAND PASS LOOP

to Hwy 135

N

Tincup

Description

Ride through Tincup on the main road, continuing straight at the four-way stop. The route climbs out of town and winds along the left side of Willow Creek. The grade is gentle and the only evidence that you're gaining elevation is expanding views of the nearby peaks. The road surface is fairly smooth except for occasional bumpy, bounce-around-on-your-seat sections. Beaver ponds dot this lush, willow-filled valley. Most of the mining around Tincup was done on the ridges to the left of the road. Keep your eyes peeled for remaining structures that dot these slopes. A short distance after the first switchback look for a well-traveled spur on the right that cuts back into the trees. Walk or bike about 0.5 miles up this road for a good view of the Blistered Horn Mill (named for its owner's sunburned nose). This 20-stamp mill serviced several mines and utilized a tram to bring ore to the site. Please observe this sturdy, well-preserved structure from the safety of the road. The mill can also be seen from above, on the main road. It's directly across from and below the large tailings dump that marks the mine site.

As you near timberline an impressive network of old mining roads crisscrossing the barren mountain slopes is visible. I kept waiting for the road to degenerate into a steep, rocky ascent characteristic of most Colorado pass roads but it never did. After about 8.5 miles of easy pedaling you reach the fairly level saddle of Cumberland Pass. There's plenty of room to spread out, relax, and enjoy views of a whole new set of mountains that are visible to the west. If you're up here on a good-weather day and have some extra time, try one or two of the tempting side roads that branch off from the saddle. The southern side of the pass is also rideable, and strong bikers could pedal over to Pitkin and back the same day.

From the top, cruise back down the same side for approximately 1.5 miles. Look for a fairly well-traveled road that forks to the right off the pass road. (You've missed it if you come to a switchback.) Take this fork and descend gradually around the side of a hill. You're now following the original route that led from Cumberland Pass into Tincup. The pass road used today wasn't constructed until the mid-1930s. Loose rock covers some of the road but it's easy to negotiate. At about 10.6 miles you reach a three-way intersection near quite a few old cabins of various shapes and sizes. The described route continues straight (left) here but take a few minutes to walk up the other fork, where additional buildings border the road.

Another junction appears almost immediately after the first one. Continue right here and ride through an open area called Duncan Flats. Still more log structures languish along the road. Extensive mining and numerous private property holdings around here make it important to stay on established routes. The many open shafts in the trees present a hidden danger. Beyond Duncan Flats the road descends more steeply as it

CUMBERLAND PASS LOOP

Ride 17

switchbacks down Duncan Hill and into a green drainage. It continues to descend along the left side of this draw. You pass a few more cabins and some tempting side roads that might be worth exploring another time. Drop into the trees and pedal over lengthy segments of rock-covered terrain. Eventually the road curves to the left and leaves the drainage behind. It merges with the bottom of Cumberland Pass Road at roughly 13.5 miles. Turn right and ride back through Tincup to your vehicle.

History

Gold panned in a tin cup by original prospectors in the Taylor Valley gave this town its name. The supposed killing of seven of its marshals within several months gave Tincup the reputation of being one of Colorado's three roughest towns. Surrounding silver and gold deposits gave it many years as a successful mining district. In 1878 the lode that later became known as Gold Cup Mine was discovered and hordes of miners arrived. By 1882 Tincup was the largest silver producer in Gunnison County and had a population of 6,000. Several devastating fires and mining recessions caused severe population fluctuations, and by 1912 Tincup's days as a boom town were over. The Gold Cup, which turned out to be the largest producer in the area, closed down in 1917.

The earliest routes into Tincup from the east were over either the gentle Cottonwood Pass or the steeper Tincup Pass. As the Pitkin mining district grew a need arose for a connection between this camp in the Quartz Creek drainage and Tincup. In 1880 a pack trail was constructed through a gap in a ridge between the two drainages and named Cumberland Pass. Two years later it was widened into a wagon road. A busy route, the pass road provided direct access to the Denver, South Park, and Pacific railway. Ore was hauled over to the train by wagon in summer and sled in winter.

As the mines above Tincup flourished more and more people flocked to the area. Located smack dab in the middle of some of the best mining, Duncan Flats became a logical place to settle. It developed in the early 1880s as miners, looking for quarters close to nearby mines, constructed cabins. Quite a few people lived in the Duncan Flats area, both working in the larger mines and operating many small ones that can be seen along the roads. Over 100 miners lived in the 25–30 cabins that were built, although a true town never really existed. Once the mines began to close in the late 1880s, the area faded and eventually was deserted.

Comments

It's a good idea to start early for this ride. You avoid the traffic (Cumberland Pass is a popular driving route) and will have plenty of time above timberline before any threatening storms roll in. Novices could also ride the Duncan Flats fork until the second junction to see the cabins but need to return the way they came. The descent along Duncan Hill is for intermediates only. Allow extra time to explore Tincup. It's a great little town with a good restaurant and small store.

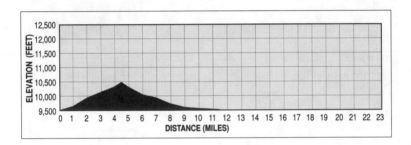

PIEPLANT

18

The first 4 miles of road to Pieplant are easy pedaling.

Location: About 39 miles north-
     east of Gunnison
Distance: 11.5 miles
Time: 3 hours
Rating: Easy*–more difficult
Low Elevation: 9,520 feet
High Point: 10,480 feet
Elevation Gain: 960 feet
Type: Loop; dirt road, single track
Season: June–October

Maps

Trails Illustrated: Pearl Pass
USFS: Gunnison
USGS County Series: Gunnison 3
USGS 7.5 Series: Pieplant

• • •

A beautifully preserved mill tucked along the base of the Collegiate Peaks and a sampling of the area's single track make this a varied ride both in its history and terrain.

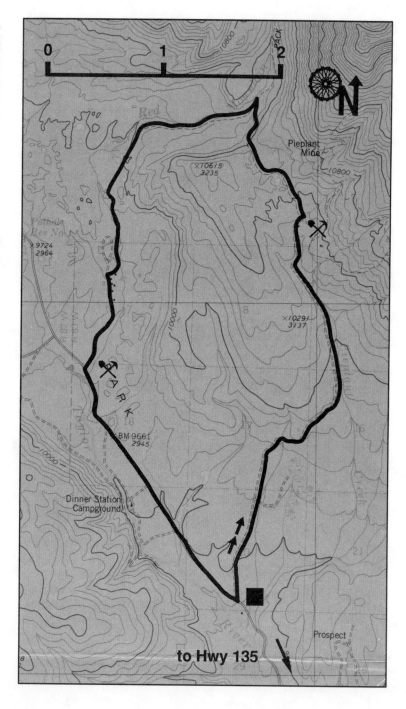

Ride **18** PIEPLANT

to Hwy 135

Access

From Gunnison drive about 11 miles north on Hwy. 135 to the junction at Almont. Take the right fork and drive about 24 miles to the pavement's end at Taylor Park Reservoir. Continue to drive up the dirt Taylor River Road for another 4 miles. Park off the road on the right by a fork for the Pieplant Road just before the main road crosses a cattle guard.

Description

Follow Pieplant Road as it climbs gradually through sagebrush toward the base of the Collegiate Peaks. These high mountains provide a breathtaking backdrop to the open meadows of Taylor Park. The first 4 miles are an excellent warmup for the trail riding. A smooth road surface and gentle gradient make pedaling a breeze. Lodgepole pine forests surround the road until it climbs to the edge of the lush Pieplant Creek drainage. A secluded meadow at the head of this drainage creates the setting for the small community of Pieplant. Quite a few cabins, both visible and concealed in the trees, are scattered throughout the area. The skeletal remains of the mill, firmly supported by a beautifully laid stonework foundation, still stand at the far edge of the meadow.

Pieplant Road basically ends at the townsite and you need to look for a small, inconspicuous sign marking the route for Timberline Trail North. The trail actually starts in between two cabins that sit under towering pines. A sign on one of the cabins reads "to Timberline Trail North." Ride between the cabins, following the trail as it curves left and up a rocky draw. After a brief walk over this rocky section you can start riding. There are more rocky sections but the trail is fairly wide, so there's room to negotiate around these technical spots. The trail climbs a bit more and then levels out. You're riding right along the edge of the Collegiate Peaks Wilderness Area; notice that any spurs forking right are marked by wilderness area boundary signs. All of these side roads are closed to mountain bikes.

Overall this part of the Timberline Trail is great riding. A few technical sections are made challenging by loose rock but this single track remains extremely rideable. You drop into a small meadow, back through the trees, and then into a larger meadow. Riding among the trees again you reach a major three-way intersection at about 5 miles. The Timberline Trail ends here, merging with the Red Mountain Trail, which forks both right and left. The Red Mountain Trail was one of the original routes used to access Taylor Park. It originated at the Arkansas River near Granite and climbed over Lake Pass before it descended along Red Mountain Creek.

Turn left at this junction and descend, following the sign for Taylor River. This trail is a little smoother, creating a delightful downhill cruise that takes you through the forest and above some beaver ponds in a meadow on the right. You'll see a few faint trail spurs in here. Stay on the main route, which is well marked by blazes on the trees. Climb briefly, then drop steeply to Red Mountain Creek. Pass a trail register box at roughly 7 miles and shortly after ford the creek. (This could be a challenge during peak runoff.) Beyond the creek the trail ends at the well-traveled Red Mountain Road. Follow this road as it drops gradually past some summer homes and after 2 miles merges with the main Taylor River Road. This intersection was the site of a busy stage stop when the roads between Tincup and Aspen bustled with mining traffic. Turn left onto the main road and cruise another 2 miles down to your vehicle.

History

Pieplants (rhubarb) growing along the edge of the creek gave this small forest community its name. Determined prospectors worked every drainage in Taylor Park and found gold in Pieplant Creek during the late 1890s. This caused only minimal excitement until parallel fissures discovered on the west side of Jenkins Mountain provided more spectacular results. A mining company was formed, a mill moved in from Leadville, and another small mining settlement took shape. The actual mine, located quite a distance above the mill in what is now wilderness area, had a tunnel bored 1,300 feet into the mountain and was about 400 feet deep. The initial operation was not very successful and in 1905 the mill shut down. Reopened later by another group, the mine operated until 1920. In addition to handling lead and silver ore from the Pieplant Mine the mill also processed ore from other mines up the Taylor River. The town was actually more of a satellite camp of larger settlements such as Dorchester and Bowman, which were established nearer to the Taylor River. About 50–60 men worked the Pieplant site and many of them inhabited the small cabins surrounding the meadow.

Little is known about the small camp of Red Mountain that was strategically situated at the base of Red Mountain Trail and along the Taylor Pass stage route. Six-shooter Brown and his wife built their ranch here and catered to the many travelers who passed through this region. The opening of nearby mines and discoveries of silver on the other side of Taylor Pass, in Aspen, only increased traffic, making the stage stop a busy place. Nothing remains of the ranch, which is now identified by a historic marker.

Comments

Watch for horse and foot traffic on the trail and remember to yield to all other users. The Timberline Trail is a fairly extensive system that runs all the way to the Tincup Pass Road. This ride explores one of the easier segments. Most of the trail receives very little maintenance and has many tough technical sections. Adventurous (and strong) bikers may enjoy the challenge it presents and with appropriately placed car shuttles could bike the entire route. Apply map-reading skills when deciding which direction to go, and allow plenty of time. Several other roads and game trails that branch off the Pieplant ride could be fun to investigate. Taylor Park has great camping, fishing, hiking, and, most important, biking. It's the perfect base for a few days of exploring. The varied terrain, ranging from smooth, flat roads to intense mountain single track, can accommodate bikers of all abilities.

Pieplant Mill sits in a meadow below the Timberline Trail.

to Hwy 50

0   1   2

Paywell Mtn
Van Wirt Mtn
Tomichi Pass
Central Mtn
Monument Pea
Granite Mountain
Stella Mtn
USLM Lamar
Tomichi Cem
Contact
USLM
Whitepine
West Point Hill
Lake Hill

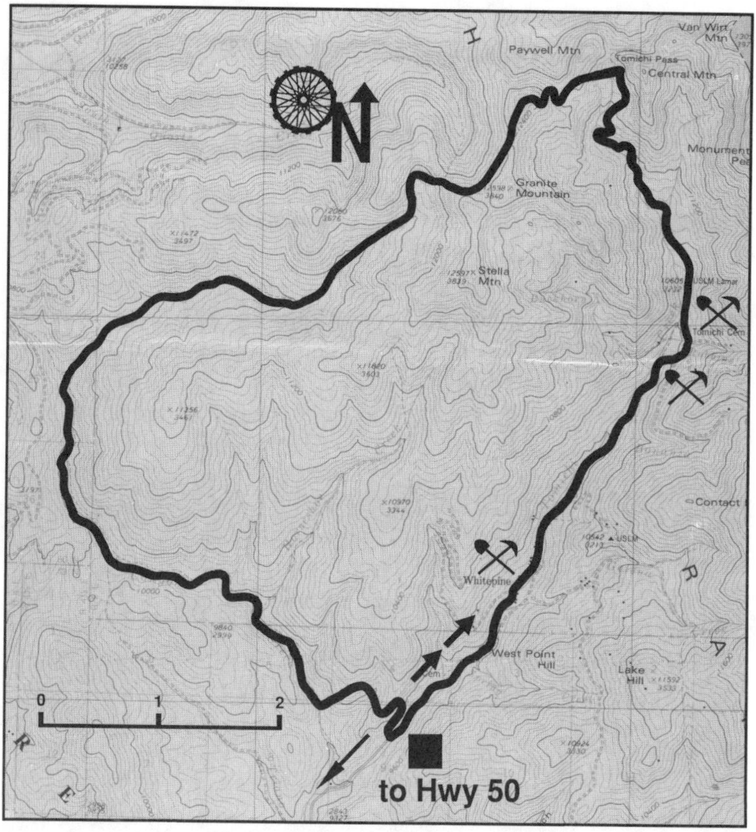

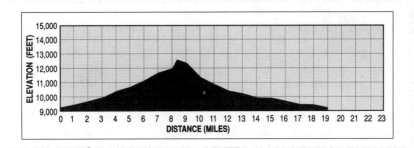

CANYON CREEK

19

Location: About 38 miles east of Gunnison
Distance: 19 miles
Time: 5–6 hours
Rating: Advanced
Low Elevation: 9,250 feet
High Point: 12,600 feet
Elevation Gain: 3,350 feet
Type: Loop; dirt road, single track
Season: Late June–September

Maps
Trails Illustrated: Shavano Peak
USFS: Gunnison
USGS County Series: Gunnison 5
USGS 7.5 Series: Garfield,
    Whitepine

• • •

Just west of the Continental Divide lies a narrow valley containing the mining districts of Whitepine and Tomichi. A scenic jeep road climbs past these sites to the beginning of Canyon Creek Trail. This outstanding single track takes riders high above timberline before it descends for miles along Canyon Creek.

Access
Drive 31 miles east of Gunnison on Hwy. 50. Just past Sargents turn left onto County Road 888 toward Whitepine. Follow this road about 7.3 miles as it turns to dirt and winds up the valley. Park near the Snowblind Campground.

Ride 19 **CANYON CREEK**

Description

Begin riding up Whitepine Road. Gradual at first, the road climbs past mining remains and through the town of Whitepine at about 2 miles. This once bustling mining camp is now a popular hunters' community. Although there are many restored and newer cabins you can still see several old buildings. Beyond Whitepine the road continues to ascend over rolling terrain. At approximately 4 miles you encounter a major three-way intersection in a small hillside meadow. Surprisingly, this empty spot once contained the large community of Tomichi, which was almost completely destroyed by an avalanche.

Take the right fork from the junction, ride past a house, and climb steeply over rocky terrain. The road curves left and crosses Robbins Creek. Just beyond the creek sits the tiny Tomichi Cemetery. It's tucked into a shady hillside meadow near the road. Some gravestones and several weathered wood crosses are scattered among the tall pines. At the junction here take the left fork that descends below the cemetery. The warmup is over and the road starts to get rougher and steeper, signaling the ascent to Tomichi Pass. The combination of steep pitches strewn with rocks makes pedaling a challenge.

At almost 7.3 miles, after the road has climbed above timberline, start looking for a difficult-to-spot trail that forks left off the road. It starts just before the road swings to the left around a small rock knob and begins its final climb to the pass. The route was marked by a small *cairn* on the side of the road and brown Forest Service markers in the meadow when I was there. Turn left onto the track, cross a small creek just below the road, and follow the Forest Service markers through a meadow. The trail curves left toward a clump of trees and becomes more obvious. It passes a small lake on the right and begins about a mile of intense climbing that requires both walking and carrying your bike. The rock-filled trail gains elevation quickly as it switchbacks toward the top of Paywell Mountain. Where the route becomes faint *cairns* mark the way. The rewards for this strenuous bike hike are some incredible views and 11 miles of downhill, all on a superb trail.

From the top the trail descends along a tundra-covered ridge and then swings around the right side of a knoll. Pass a trail that drops in from the left and continue to contour until you reach a junction at roughly 9 miles. Several weathered trail signs mark this intersection. Take the most heavily traveled trail, which drops into a large drainage to the west. Traverse the head of the valley and swing down into the right side of the drainage. Now the real fun begins as the trail drops quickly along the right side of Canyon Creek. Almost completely rideable, it is characterized by long, smooth sections occasionally broken up by some technical spots containing rocks, roots, or bogs.

At about 13.3 miles you pass through a horse outfitter's camp and encounter a junction. Turn left and cross over the creek on a footbridge. Continue to descend, now along the left side of the creek, and pass an old road that forks to the left. This section of trail is even smoother but has a few sandy spots. At almost 15 miles you come to another signed junction. Take the left fork toward Sargents. This next segment of trail is my favorite. It seems made just for bikes as it meanders through trees and descends around tight turns along the left side of the creek. After dropping into a tall grass meadow the trail becomes rocky for a brief period and crosses a tiny creek. It then heads back into the trees and continues to descend. Beyond a cabin foundation you encounter a fork to the left for Horseshoe Creek Trail. Continue straight on the Canyon Creek Trail.

All good things come to an end, and at almost 17.7 miles a junction marks the beginning of a short, steep climb. The trail forks sharply left near a sign on a tree. Do not continue straight or you'll end up on private property. Leaving the creek, you climb along a small draw. The trail switchbacks to the right and climbs around a ridge. It gets steep and you may have to do a little pushing to reach the high point. You get a final long-distance view back to the mountains you ascended earlier before a thrilling, switchback-filled descent to your vehicle.

History

The first mining claims, rich in lead and silver, were staked in this area during 1878–1879. The Northstar, east of Whitepine in Galena Gulch, became one of the most valuable properties in western Colorado. In 1880 the first store was opened, and Whitepine was formally laid out in 1881. This single-street town had over 1,000 residents at one time, and a variety of stores crowded the main thoroughfare. Whitepine was virtually inaccessible during winter, when the only route out toward Sargents was often clogged with snow. Sleds were used to remove ore in the winter months. The town actually experienced three separate boom periods, with some of the mines producing until 1952. The *White Pine Cone*, a local newspaper, was famous for its thorough reports and witty entries including such tidbits as, "The boys all washed their feet in the Hot Springs Sunday. There will be no fish in Hot Springs Creek this summer."

The empty spot where Tomichi once stood is a stark contrast to the boisterous camp that once lined the hillside. In 1880 it was larger than Whitepine, with a population of 1,500. The Magna Charta, the largest mine in the area, had a large tunnel that stretched through Granite Mountain for over a mile. After the silver crash of 1893 Tomichi was deserted but experienced a small revival by 1896. In 1899 a devastating avalanche

CANYON CREEK

Ride 19

obliterated most of the town, destroyed mining equipment, and killed several people. Survivors, afraid of more snowslides, moved to Whitepine. Any salvageable buildings were carted away and only a secluded cemetery and an open space on the hillside mark any evidence of this once booming camp.

Comments

The mile of climbing to Paywell Mountain is one of the toughest I've done. Attempt this ride only if you're capable of pushing/carrying your bike up steep stretches of trail. Keep a sharp eye out for horse parties, which frequent this area, and remember to give them the right-of-way. This ride should only be attempted on guaranteed good-weather days since you are above timberline for a long time. If you ride here during the fall use extra caution and wear colorful clothing since the area is frequented by hunters.

Rides Around Crested Butte

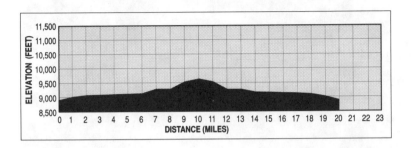

POVERTY GULCH

20

The first 8 miles are an easy pedal, while the Poverty Gulch Road is a bit more challenging.

Location: Crested Butte
Distance: 20 miles
Time: 3–4 hours
Rating: Easy*–moderate
Low Elevation: 8,900 feet
High Point: 9,600 feet
Elevation Gain: 700 feet
Type: Out and back; dirt road, pavement
Season: Late May–October

Maps
Trails Illustrated: Pearl Pass, Kebler Pass West
USFS: Gunnison
USGS County Series: Gunnison 2
USGS 7.5 Series: Oh-Be-Joyful, Gothic, Crested Butte

• • •

The delightful combination of riverside riding, hillside wildflower havens, towering mountains, and easy pedaling terrain makes this a great introduction to mountain biking around Crested Butte.

Access
Drive into Crested Butte. Park in the large lot by the tennis courts near the four-way stop.

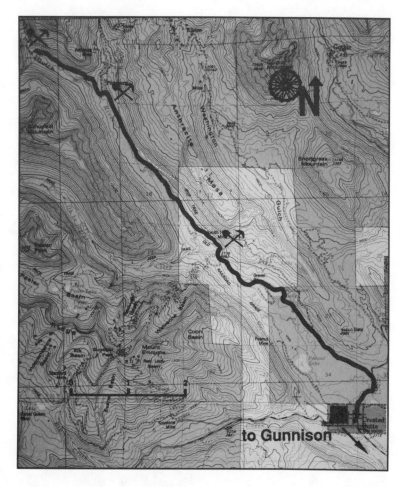

to Gunnison

Description

From the four-way stop, continue straight on 6th Avenue toward Mt. Crested Butte. Follow the paved road for about 0.5 miles, passing a cemetery. Turn left onto dirt Road 734 and pedal up the Slate River. Other than occasional overdoses of gravel, this road has a smooth surface that allows for plenty of rubbernecking at Crested Butte's spectacular mountains. A few homes and the Peanut Mine workings, perched on a hill on the left side of the river, occupy the wide mouth of this drainage. Grazing cows wander freely and you'll have plenty of opportunities to test different techniques for passing them. A calm, slow approach seems to work the best.

Beyond Nicholson Lake the valley narrows a bit and you ride deeper into the mountains bordering this drainage. Pass a fork to the left for Gunsight Pass, an advanced ride, at a little over 4 miles. The grade you can see down by the river was a spur of the Denver and Rio Grande Railroad that ended just upriver. Look above to the hillside on the right to see the Smith Hill Mine, one of the few remaining intact mines in this area. The next spur you pass leads up Oh-Be-Joyful Creek and is a recommended intermediate ride. The road continues at the same pace and climbs very gradually over rolling terrain. Crested Butte is in the heart of wildflower country and during midsummer grassy hillside meadows along this drainage are filled with color.

At about 8 miles you pass a sign notifying you of the private property around Pittsburg. Once a mining town, it now supports a few private residences. Just ahead is the fork to the left for Poverty Gulch. The easy pedaling ends here; however, the road into Poverty Gulch would only be challenging to someone brand new to the sport. If you are turning around at Pittsburg but plan to take a rest stop before you descend, be sure to choose a spot outside of the area marked as private property.

To continue on the described route turn left at the junction. (The main road begins to climb much more steeply toward Washington Gulch and Paradise Divide.) Ford a stream and pass a couple of driveways. Climb moderately for about 0.5 miles over somewhat rocky terrain. The road then levels off and you begin a more gradual climb along the right side of the gulch. This area seems much wilder and less disturbed than the main drainage, although it was once crawling with miners. As you ride toward the base of Cascade Mountain the feathery waterfalls that stream down its cliffs become visible.

The road eventually curves right and climbs to a more rugged section of the drainage near an old tailings dump. The terrain gets much rougher and the ride basically ends here. You may not want to ride any farther, but drop your bike and walk a short distance to a flat spot above the tailings. From here you experience an exquisite visual combination: a series of

POVERTY GULCH

Ride 20

waterfalls that cascade into a thick field of wildflowers. This is a great place to spend some time. The road that forks left from a junction climbs steeply to Daisy Pass and is appropriate only for advanced riders or hikers. You can barely see the right fork, which climbs the cliffs to the right of Cascade Mountain and accesses Augusta Mine. Once you've had your fill of the scenery, return as you came.

History

Although the initial mining around Crested Butte was done in search of valuable ore, it was coal that supported the population of this town after hardrock mining diminished. The Peanut and Smith Hill mines were both coal producers. These mines, and others in the area, contained the only known anthracite coal west of Pennsylvania. A spur of the Denver and Rio Grande Railroad up the Slate River provided more efficient shipping of the coal from these mines, but this extension was only open a few months each year due to the hazard of avalanches and the difficulty of clearing snowdrifts. Smith Hill was a large operation that shipped 10 to 20 railroad cars of coal daily during the 1880s. It employed over 200 men, who lived in nearby cabins.

Pittsburg was laid out in 1880 and boomed the following year when successful silver strikes were made in Poverty Gulch. Soon after, a post office was established, and by 1886 the population of about 200 warranted daily stage service to Crested Butte. The Augusta Mine was the big producer in this area. Its large vein contained gold, silver, and lead that was rumored to be the richest in the nation. Tough to get to, it was accessible only on foot or by horseback, and work crews stayed at the mine all winter without coming out. The Augusta went through several successful and disastrous periods including the silver panic of 1893 and a destructive avalanche that wiped out the mill, the tram, and some mine buildings. Over $1 million in silver ore was produced before final closure in the early 1900s. Due to the continual danger of snowslides between Crested Butte and Pittsburg, the town was mainly a summer community. Inaccessibility and the closure of nearby mines led to its eventual decline.

Comments

You may encounter some traffic although I saw more mountain bikers than anything else. Please respect the private property signs around Pittsburg. These folks must be overwhelmed by the amount of two-wheeled traffic that passes their homes. Several intermediate and advanced ride options originate from Slate River Road.

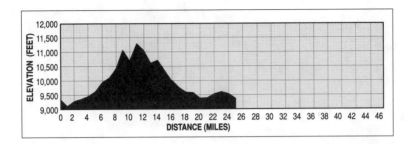

PARADISE DIVIDE

21

*A few steep climbs and the lengthy elevation gain necessitate the more difficult rating. However, a physically strong, moderate rider could complete the entire ride since little technical skill is needed.

Location: Crested Butte
Distance: 25 miles
Time: 4–5 hours
Rating: Moderate*–more difficult
Low Elevation: 9,120 feet
High Point: 11,280 feet
Elevation Gain: 2,160 feet
Type: Loop; dirt road, pavement
Season: Late June–early October

Maps
Trails Illustrated: Pearl Pass, Kebler
  Pass West
USFS: Gunnison, White River
USGS County Series: Gunnison 2
USGS 7.5 Series: Oh-Be-Joyful,
  Gothic, Snowmass Mountain

• • •

The name of this ride sums it up nicely. You're in mountain-bike paradise the entire time. Challenging climbs, fast descents, an alpine lake nestled on the divide, and massive fields of wildflowers all combine to make this a great backcountry biking experience.

Access
From Crested Butte continue straight at the four-way intersection toward Mt. Crested Butte. Drive to the ski area. Turn right onto Treasury Road and park in the large parking area on the right.

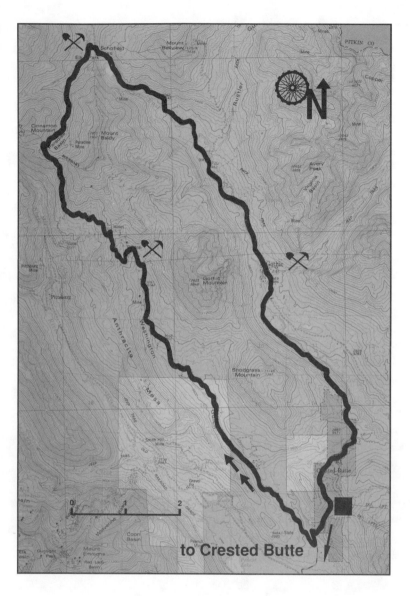

to Crested Butte

Description

Ride back down the paved road for a little over a mile and turn right onto County Road 811. Follow this well-maintained road up Washington Gulch. The gravel doesn't last for long, nor do the houses. After passing a lake you encounter a three-way intersection. Take the left fork, cross a cattle guard, and pedal up along the side of the valley.

Beyond this point the road becomes less used and more suitable for mountain biking. You wind in and out of the trees and through meadows that are thick with wildflowers in July. It's worth it to carry a camera on this ride, although it's difficult to catch the essence of riding among waist-high Queen Anne's lace and daisies. Beyond an A-frame you begin some staircase climbing, with steeper sections tempered by level recovery areas. The hillsides become more thickly forested and the flowers get even better.

A switchback to the left at about 8 miles passes below a cabin that sits perched above the road. The next mile has some lung-bursting pitches as it climbs past another restored cabin on a wildflower-covered knoll. Elkton, a small town of which few traces remain, sat between this cabin and the first one you saw. Switchback left near Painter Boy Mine, marked by the carcass of an old truck, and climb to a small divide at approximately 9 miles. A sign here for Trail 403 (a great advanced ride) identifies a fork to the right. Continue on the main road, descending for a little over a mile to a junction. Turn right and begin the climb to Paradise Divide. This ascent is not as steep as the grade near Elkton and once again is broken up with some fairly level sections. Besides, the views are enough to make anyone forget about the energy they're exerting. High peaks in all directions provide a welcome distraction until you reach Paradise Divide, at just over 11 miles. A small pond at the saddle is the perfect place to sit and soak up the views.

From the divide you drop into green cirques surrounding Paradise Basin. Pass some side roads that look like good exploring and descend into the open meadows of Elko Park. Look carefully in this area and you may spot some cabin foundations that remain from small settlements that once developed here. The road curves to the right and climbs for a while until it reaches Schofield Pass at about 14 miles. Another great single track, Trail 401, takes off from here (see "Additional Rides in Region 3").

Following another drainage containing more spectacular views, you swoop down along the East River as it descends around jewel-like Emerald Lake, through a deeply carved canyon, and into meadows that line its banks. Though it's tempting to really fly on this downhill cruise all the way to Gothic, you need to be extra cautious of traffic. Excellent road conditions mean even the family wagon can inch its way along this route, so be alert, especially on the narrower sections.

This route takes you right along the main street of Gothic. Ride slowly and be observant to see many older buildings that have been restored and added on to. One classic old structure now serves as a store and sells snacks, including ice cream!! Beyond Gothic you have about 5 more miles of riding. The first bit is a gradual climb, and then it's all downhill as the road turns to pavement and descends to the ski area.

History

The area above Crested Butte began to attract prospectors in the 1850s and 1860s. However, important mineral discoveries weren't made until around 1880. Then the boom was on. Elkton came into existence at this time and sported a store, hotel, and the ever-present post office. By 1882, at least 17 mines were working in the area. The Painter Boy, which contained a lot of high-grade silver, became a dominant producer with over $100,000 in silver ore. By the late 1880s the town was almost deserted, and a fire in 1893 destroyed the majority of its buildings.

High in the meadows of Elko Park the small mining camp of Elko struggled for survival in a harsh climate. Men working their way up from Gothic found silver deposits at the base of Galena Mountain and established the camp that grew into Elko. Short-lived at first, the settlement experienced renewed interest in 1901 and a 3,000-foot tunnel was dug into Galena Mountain. But the town's distance from the nearest market and the questionable value of the ore led to desertion of this community.

Schofield Pass has always been a busy place. Today full of bikers, hikers, and jeepers, it was once a major route between the mining towns of Marble, Crystal, Gothic, and Crested Butte. Gothic was the first settlement that travelers coming from the west side saw. The Sylvanite Mine, located at the head of Copper Creek, contained silver ore so rich it ran over $15,000 a ton. This news brought fortune seekers and in 1879 Gothic was established. Growth came quickly; a smelter was built, and talk of railroad service began. The peak population was thought to be around 5,000 and a school, stores, restaurants, hotels, and saloons soon crowded the area. But silver discoveries in the surrounding mountains never met the high expectations and even the Sylvanite was closed by 1885. People began leaving and Gothic would have become a complete ghost town except for its rescue by the Rocky Mountain Biological Laboratory, which runs classes, conferences, and research on and around the site.

Comments

Allow plenty of time for this ride. There are a variety of side explorations and a lot of wonderful spots for peak gazing, wildflower viewing, and naps in the sun. Getting an early start should also put you ahead of thunderstorms that could be dangerous when you're above timberline on Paradise Divide. This ride takes you through wildflower heaven. To take advantage of this, visit Crested Butte in mid-July when the blossoms peak.

Rides Around Aspen

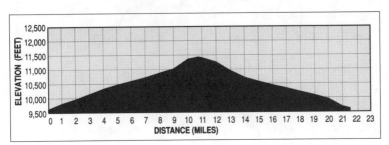

RUBY

22

*Beyond Grizzly Reservoir the road gets rocky. However, the continuation of a gradual grade makes this section manageable for someone who's had a little technical experience.

Location: About 10 miles south-east of Aspen
Distance: 21.5 miles
Time: 4–5 hours
Rating: Moderate*–more difficult
Low Elevation: 9,600 feet
High Point: 11,440 feet
Elevation Gain: 1,840 feet
Type: Out and back; dirt road
Season: June–October

Maps
Trails Illustrated: Independence Pass
USFS: White River
USGS County Series: Pitkin 2
USGS 7.5 Series: Independence Pass, New York Peak

• • •

A gradual, relatively painless climb along Lincoln Creek accesses a striking high alpine meadow that surrounds the ghost town of Ruby. Plenty of peaks, wildflowers, and interesting buildings highlight this historic tour.

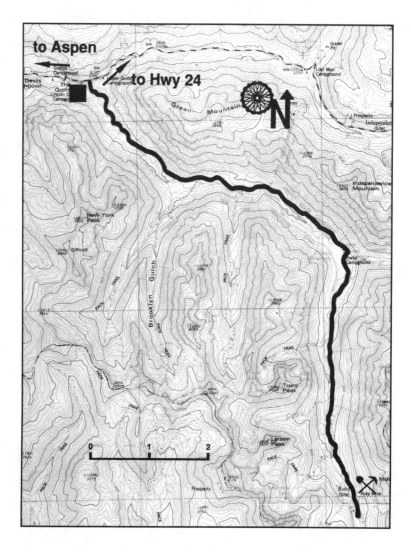

to Aspen

to Hwy 24

N

Access

From Aspen, drive 9.6 miles southeast on Hwy. 82 toward Independence Pass. Turn right onto Lincoln Creek Road. Cross the bridge and drive down a short distance to the campground. Park in the small pullouts at the beginning of the campground road, or drive a little farther on the main road and park in one of the many pullouts.

Description

This ride is unique in that it allows you to view the classic beauty of Colorado's high basins without the exhausting climbs it usually takes to get to them. Lincoln Creek Road is in pretty good shape up to Grizzly Reservoir. About half a mile of fairly level warmup is followed by about a mile of staircase riding that consists of short, steep climbs with plenty of flat recovery areas. There are very few technical spots so even the climbs are extremely rideable. The road meanders along the edge of Lincoln Creek, which alternates between placid pools and frothing drops through boulder-choked channels.

At about 2.8 miles you pass York Creek trailhead on the right. The road levels out beyond this point for some pleasant pedaling through open meadows and shady forests surrounded by soaring peaks. You pass another trailhead about a mile farther up the road and reach Grizzly Reservoir at approximately 6 miles. Ride around the left side of the lake, pass the Portal Campground, and continue pedaling up Lincoln Gulch. Beyond the reservoir the road receives no maintenance and contains a lot more rock. You scarcely know you're climbing because the grade is so minimal, but you do need some technical ability to negotiate the sections of rock you frequently encounter.

The road travels through large open meadows and small clumps of pine. There are a few stream crossings and some steeper stretches as you work your way up the valley. Once the head of the gulch gets closer keep your eyes peeled for old cabins. Quite a few are hidden in the trees or down near the banks of Lincoln Creek. After pedaling a little over 9 miles you reach the outskirts of Ruby. An interpretive sign highlighting the area's history sits to the left of the road. The owners of this land, instead of exercising their option to close off the area, hired a caretaker to watch over the old townsite while still allowing public access. Respect their request to stay on the road and steer clear of all private property.

More and more remains of Ruby appear. Some structures have signs describing their origin. When you pass some new homes belonging to the landowner, look for a mine situated near their front yard. It was one of the top producers in this district. Beyond their house the head of the valley opens up and several other mines are visible on the hillside to your left. The

RUBY

Ride 22

brilliant rust-colored mountain above these mines, logically named Red Mountain, once had a pack trail going over it that connected with routes leading to Leadville. Some of this path is still visible on the lower part of the mountain. The road ends near the farthest cabins, which are marked by a private property sign. The cabin that's had some restoration work done on it is the caretaker's residence.

If you want to do some more exploring while in this valley, descend back through Ruby and look for a road farther down the valley that forks to the left. It crosses Lincoln Creek and disappears into the trees by a hillside cabin. A quick hike takes you up this road to a couple of high alpine lakes. The smoothness of the lower Lincoln Gulch Road is a relief after the bumpy descent from Ruby. It's easy to get your speed up so be cautious around blind corners. Keep an eye out for vehicles and other bikers.

History

Several veins of silver were discovered near the head of Lincoln Creek by exploring prospectors who wandered over Green Mountain from the town of Independence. A few different camps were set up near timberline, which led to the use of various names for these high country settlements. The Lincoln Mining District was formed in September 1880. Local mines were good producers but ore had to be packed by mule train over Red Mountain into the South Fork of Lake Creek and eventually on to Leadville. It was this rigorous journey that initially kept Ruby from really booming. It took too much effort and expense to transport the ore.

In the early 1900s the Ruby Mining and Development Company began operations in the gulch. The community settled on the name of Ruby, a wagon road was built from the Roaring Fork Road, and mining in the district thrived. The company erected a 50-ton concentrating plant and bored a long tunnel under Red Mountain. Silver, gold, lead, iron, and a little molybdenum were taken from this area. The Ruby Mining Company closed its operation in 1912 and only a few diehard miners remained to work their claims.

Comments

This road has traffic, mainly on weekends and mainly to the reservoir. A good approach to this ride is to start early and spend most of the day in the Ruby area. Return in late afternoon when traffic has subsided some.

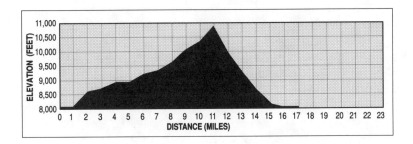

LEAD KING BASIN

23

*Although much of this ride re-
quires solid physical and technical
abilities, the section to Crystal can
be pedaled by intermediate riders.*

Location: About 28 miles south of
 Carbondale
Distance: 17 miles
Time: 5 hours
Rating: Moderate–more difficult*
Low Elevation: 8,000 feet
High Point: 10,800 feet
Elevation Gain: 2,800 feet
Type: Loop, out and back; dirt road
Season: Late June–October

Maps
Trails Illustrated: Maroon Bells
USFS: White River
USGS County Series: Gunnison 1
USGS 7.5 Series: Marble,
 Snowmass Mountain

• • •

Skirting around the rugged Elk Mountains, Lead King Basin Road takes
bikers past the peaceful old town of Crystal and into a pristine high alpine
basin. Miles of pedaling along the vividly colored Crystal River enhance
the already spectacular surroundings.

Access

From Aspen, drive west on Hwy. 82 until you reach Carbondale. Turn south
onto Hwy. 133 and follow it for 22 miles to the turnoff for Marble. Turn left
onto County Road 3 and drive another 5.6 miles to Marble. Turn right near
the private campground and park in the large lot near the river. (The county
road is undergoing improvements, so access directions may change somewhat.)

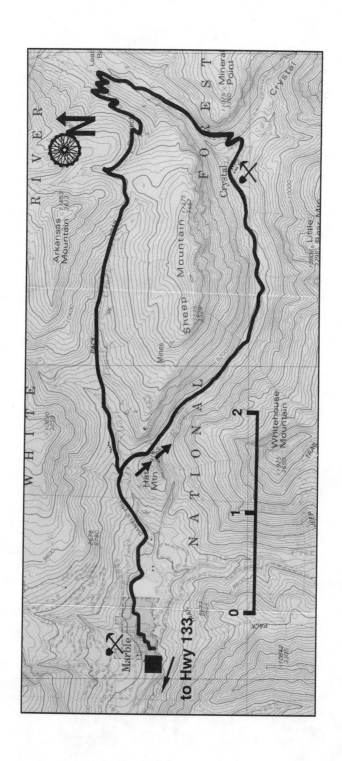

Description

Ride through Marble. Follow the semi-paved main road that jogs left and then right near a church. Cross a bridge, continue weaving through town, and curve right at a sign for Crystal City, where the road turns to dirt. Pedal past Beaver Lake and begin climbing. Several small hills provide a warmup before a mile of more difficult climbing that ascends Daniels Hill. Although not very technical, this climb is taxing because it never lets up. At the top there's a junction. The left fork, marked for Lead King Basin, is where you come out later. Take the right fork toward Crystal. Drop down to and cross Lost Trail Creek. Climb up from the creek, pass Lizard Lake, and descend to the Crystal River.

The next couple of miles of riding alternate between short climbs and descents and relaxing riding along the banks of the Crystal River. Deep pools, tinted in various shades of green, look like inviting places for a swim if you're pedaling on a hot day. At almost 6 miles you pass the picturesque Crystal Mill that sits above the river. Beyond the mill, situated in a meadow between two forks of the Crystal River, is the quiet town of Crystal. Restored buildings support a few residents and a small store. Those who turn around here should ride a short distance past town to the first switchback. A small grassy area near a crystal-clear pond makes a perfect lunch spot.

To continue the ride, switchback left on the road and climb through a shady grove of aspen. Noticeably rougher and steeper, the road contains a lot of loose rock, making traction a hit-or-miss situation. You may end up walking a bit. A junction appears at roughly 6.7 miles. Take a sharp left toward Lead King Basin. (The right fork goes to Schofield Pass.) For a while the road gets even rockier, which means one small error and you're walking again. But this doesn't last long and the slow pace gives you a chance to appreciate the narrow, steeply walled canyon created by the North Fork of the Crystal. The views only get better, and if you can take your eyes off the rocky obstacle course you're negotiating you'll appreciate the stunning beauty of peak-rimmed Lead King Basin.

The farther into the basin you ride, the fewer rocks there are, although some technical spots still test your skills. The road climbs into a meadow and across the river and passes a small cabin at roughly 8 miles. Beyond this point the terrain becomes much smoother. Pass a trailhead parking area on the right and begin about 2.5 miles of climbing. A lot of elevation is gained as the road switchbacks up to the high point, but I was pleasantly surprised by the ease of this climb. The road surface is excellent and there's always a long recovery area after each steep section. In addition, around every switchback there's a completely different perspective of the basin, including waterfalls, wildflower-covered slopes, and high ridges covered in deep cornices of snow.

LEAD KING BASIN

The high point is reached at about 11 miles. The main road curves left and a spur climbs steeply up a hill. When I was there a thick blanket of daisies covered the hillside. Take the spur a short distance to be immersed in this wildflower jungle and to find a unique lunch site. From this spot the main road descends into a pine forest. A long downhill is sure to bring a big grin to your face. A smooth road surface and tight switchbacks drop you into a heavily forested drainage. Farther down expect to negotiate several rocky sections. After passing the Colorado Outward Bound site on the right, the road descends a bit more to the junction on Daniels Hill. From here, backtrack to Marble and your vehicle. Be extra cautious of traffic on the final descent. Before leaving the sleepy community of Marble take some time to pedal its streets and explore the old mill site by the river. The town has a wonderful character, made unique by the huge slabs of marble that clutter the roadsides.

Ride 23

History

Prospectors looking for gold and silver were the first settlers in this valley, but it was nearby marble deposits that fueled Marble's existence. Once the value of this pure white stone was fully realized, the town boomed. Incorporated in 1899, it grew to around 1,500 residents by the early 1900s and then began a boom and bust cycle caused by a collapse in the marble market during World Wars I and II. The quarry closed twice, in 1917 and again in 1941. After the second closure only a handful of residents remained in town. The quarry lies about 4 miles south of Marble, but the mill (the largest of its kind in the world) was built right along the river's edge. An electric trolley brought stone down the mountain to the mill. Buildings constructed completely or partially from this marble include the Tomb of the Unknown Soldier and the Washington and Lincoln monuments. During the summer of 1990 the quarry was being reopened. Road improvements and growth in town are sure to follow, with a new chapter in this town's history about to be written.

Miners exploring regions beyond Schofield Pass found rich silver ore around Crystal during 1880. Named for the crystal-like quartz found in those diggings, Crystal started as a small settlement to support men working nearby mines. By 1886 a permanent population of around 100 lived in this scenic valley. One of the first and most prosperous mines around Crystal was the Lead King, located in the meadow at the edge of Lead King Basin. Initially the ore from this site was packed over Schofield Pass by mule to be milled in Gothic. To cut down on the costs of this expensive operation a mill was later erected near the mine. Still, the lack of a road to the lower valley from Crystal made mining in this area an expensive proposition, and much of the mineral wealth in Lead King Basin was never tapped. The Lead King was worked off and on until the early 1900s. After the road from Crystal to Marble was built in 1883, the population swelled. However, the ebb and flow of the mining industry affected Crystal, and by the early 1900s only a few residents remained. Built in 1893, the beautifully preserved mill located on the edge of town contained a water wheel that turned an air compressor and powered a stamp mill and sawmill. The last time this mill operated was during 1916, when the reopening of two mines was considered.

Comments

Riders going only to Crystal can avoid the Daniels Hill climb by driving to the top and parking at the junction. Don't try this in a gutless vehicle. Also, the first few miles of road have a longer season and can be ridden by early June. Marble gets quite a few tourists on weekends, but beyond Crystal the traffic drops to almost nothing. The last few miles of climbing are quite exposed and should be avoided during bad weather.

Located near the trailhead are remains of the enormous mill, which processed marble from a nearby quarry.

ADDITIONAL RIDES IN
REGION 3
• • •

Hartmans Rocks
The granite outcrops of Hartmans Rocks provide a spectacular backdrop to the variety of bikeable terrain on this sagebrush plateau. The lower, drier setting creates a much longer riding season. Situated just south of Gunnison, Hartmans Rocks are accessed from the paved county road that travels behind the airport. An 8-mile moderate loop follows the main road, which climbs steeply up the front side of the ridge, passes through a gate, and continues climbing to the high point near several rock outcrops. From here it cuts through the sagebrush to a three-way junction. Follow the right fork, which descends along a cottonwood-lined draw. At the bottom, turn left and follow this fork to another junction, where you turn left again. A moderate climb up another green drainage brings you back onto the sagebrush flats. To loop back to the main road, fork left at the junction just past a gate and pedal across the plateau until you reach the original junction. From here you backtrack to the paved road. You'll probably notice an enticing amount of trails and roads branching off this ride. The folks at The Tune Up bike shop in Gunnison can provide other riding suggestions.

Alpine Tunnel–West Portal
The western approach to the Alpine Tunnel follows a railroad grade above timberline and into a gulch where the tunnel was constructed. Interpretive signs, historic ruins, and a close-up glimpse of the collapsed tunnel entrance make this a great ride for any railroad buff. The best place to start pedaling the grade (now a dirt road) is a few miles beyond Pitkin (27 miles northeast of Gunnison) at the junction for Cumberland Pass. This easy 20.5-mile ride forks right from the junction and climbs gradually. You pass old water tanks and remains from small mining camps and pedal along the steep cliffs of Mt. Poor to reach the tunnel site.

Italian Creek
Italian Creek Road climbs from the Taylor River into a remote valley full of wildflowers and enclosed by looming peaks. It originates about 48 miles northeast of Gunnison in the Taylor Park area. A more difficult 7.7-mile climb brings you to an exposed saddle where you have spectacular views of

the Collegiate Peaks. The many small meadows just below the saddle make great lunch spots. Although the road actually continues into the Cement Creek drainage and comes out near Crested Butte, I recommend that you return the way you came unless you have a shuttle set up. Please respect the "No Trespassing" signs near the several small houses up this drainage.

Cement Creek

The road up Cement Creek accommodates all abilities of bikers. Beginning about 7 miles southeast of Crested Butte, this ride starts out gradually and gets progressively more difficult as it climbs deep into the surrounding mountains. Lively Cement Creek parallels the route, which crosses waving fields of wildflowers. After 13 miles the road basically ends at the base of a rugged cirque. Additional exploration is possible on several side roads and trails taking off from this drainage.

Trail 401

Advanced riders will enjoy Trail 401, a classic Crested Butte single track. This 13.5-mile loop starts from a trailhead parking lot just beyond Gothic. Most of the elevation is gained by climbing for approximately 5 miles along the main road to reach Schofield Pass. The trail takes off from the right side of the pass. After about 20 minutes of intensely steep bike hiking you break out into high alpine meadows and head back toward Gothic. The next 7 miles are a single-track descent consisting of smooth hillside riding, numerous stream crossings, and technical sections full of roots and rocks. The trail ends at a dirt road that takes you back down to the roadside parking above Gothic.

Reno Divide–Deadman Pass Loop

Another superb Crested Butte trail, this ride starts about 7 miles up Cement Creek Road, which is accessed about 7 miles southeast of Crested Butte. Find a good place to park (avoid pullouts marked with private property signs) and ride up Cement Creek Road. Fork right onto Reno Divide Road and climb for roughly 4 miles until you reach the divide. Just beyond the fence turn right onto a trail that descends along Flag Creek. After about 3 miles of downhill turn right onto Trail 426, which climbs for a few more miles up another drainage. At the head of this valley the trail veers left onto a logging road, which you follow a short distance until you turn onto Bear Creek Trail. After another great descent the trail merges with Deadmans Gulch. Turn right and ride up this gulch to a forested saddle. The final descent takes you, via numerous switchbacks, to Cement Creek, which you have to ford before you get back on the main road. Single-track lovers will want to do this advanced 19.3-mile loop over and over.

Rio Grande Trail

Starting in Aspen, the Rio Grande Trail is an ideal ride for first-time mountain bikers. Accessed across from the Aspen post office, the route is a paved bike trail for the first 2 miles before it crosses a road and turns into a wide single track. Following the old railroad grade, the trail descends gently along cottonwood-lined banks of the Roaring Fork River. It eventually ends at a junction on a sagebrush plateau about 6 miles downriver, where you have several options. The left fork descends to Woody Creek bridge and follows the paved Upper River Road to Woody Creek Tavern, a great lunch spot. The right fork takes you onto the paved McClain Flats Road, which loops back into town. Or you can simply return as you came.

Smuggler–Hunter Area

Another ride that begins right in Aspen, the Smuggler-Hunter area offers many biking options over moderate–more difficult terrain. A fun 8.5-mile loop starts with a climb up a jeep road up the west side of Smuggler Mountain. From a junction at the top of the climb follows the left fork, which drops into Hunter Creek drainage. Once in this small valley you ride to a bridge that crosses Hunter Creek. Several options exist from this point, but to complete the suggested loop take the trail that forks left before the bridge and descends along the left side of the creek. Alternating between single track and old road, this route eventually crosses a bridge high over Hunter Creek and drops onto a paved road in a subdivision above Aspen. Descend along this paved road to return to town.

Richmond Hill

This wonderful ridgetop tour offers miles of advanced, above-timberline riding. A strenuous ascent up Little Annie Road (located just north of Aspen up Castle Creek Road) climbs along the back side of Aspen Mountain. It connects with Richmond Hill Road south of the mountaintop restaurant. From this point the route travels for over 10 miles along the ridge. A series of challenging climbs and descents brings you into high alpine meadows. The ridgetop road connects this 24-mile loop by dropping down onto Taylor Pass. From the pass you descend back to Castle Creek Road and come out at the old townsite of Ashcroft.

Hay Park

Lush green meadows, dense aspen groves, and spectacular views of Mt. Sopris and the Elk Range make this moderate–more difficult ride particularly scenic. Trailhead parking on Dinkle Lake Road is accessed from either Carbondale or Basalt. This 8-mile ride is steep and rocky at first and then levels out as it passes the Thomas Lakes Trail and drops into the first of many beautiful aspen groves. Alternating between road and single track, the route crosses a stream and meanders through groves of aspen and pine into meadows. A grassy hilltop bisected by a fence marks the turn-around point. The trail actually continues to Capitol Creek Road, but a good map and detailed directions are needed to follow the route.

Ivanhoe Lake Loop

A variety of the terrain around Hagerman Pass is explored in this 25-mile easy–more difficult ride. Drive about 31 miles east of Basalt, pass Ruedi Reservoir, and park at the pavement's end where Hagerman Pass Road begins. Follow this dirt road as it climbs along the old railroad grade toward Hagerman Pass. Fork right at Ivanhoe Lake and stay on the grade, which winds around the lake. Where the road splits again, leave the railroad grade, descend into a beautiful meadow, and ride around the edge of Lily Pad Lake. (Novice riders will want to turn around here.) Beyond this small lake the road eventually deteriorates into a wide single track and begins a steep, rocky descent into the Fryingpan River drainage. You end up on a well-maintained road that loops back to Hagerman Pass Road.

Bikeable Passes

Of the many passes in Region 3, those that are bikeable include Black Sage, Waunita, Tomichi, Cumberland, Taylor, Pearl, Schofield, Gunsight, Kebler, and Ohio. Lower elevations and gradual grades on some of these passes make them great for novices. Several passes make ideal two-day trips with overnights in Crested Butte or Aspen.

Region 4
San Juans

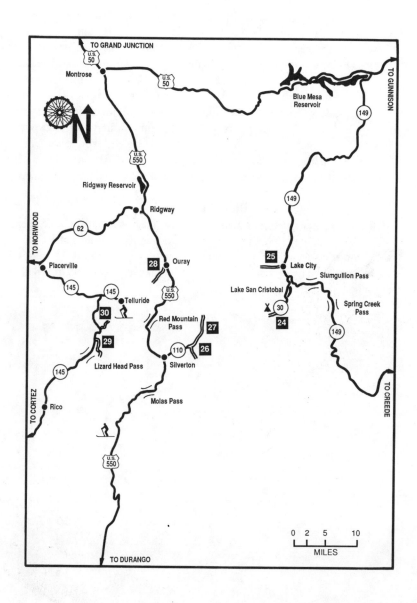

TO GRAND JUNCTION

Montrose

U.S. 50

U.S. 50

Blue Mesa Reservoir

TO GUNNISON

149

U.S. 550

Ridgway Reservoir

Ridgway

149

TO NORWOOD

62

Placerville

28 Ouray

25 Lake City

Slumgullion Pass

145

145

Telluride

U.S. 550

Lake San Cristobal

30

Spring Creek Pass

30

Red Mountain Pass

27

24

149

29

110

26

TO CORTEZ

145

Lizard Head Pass

Silverton

TO CREEDE

Rico

Molas Pass

U.S. 550

TO DURANGO

0 2 5 10

MILES

Rides Around Lake City

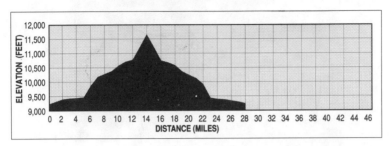

AMERICAN BASIN

24

The first 5.5 miles, up to the junction near the Sherman townsite, are an easy ride.

Location: About 8.7 miles southwest of Lake City
Distance: 28 miles
Time: 5–6 hours
Rating: Easy*–more difficult
Low Elevation: 9,200 feet
High Point: 11,600 feet
Elevation Gain: 2,400 feet
Type: Out and back; dirt road
Season: Late May–October

Maps
Trails Illustrated: none for this region
USFS: Gunnison
USGS County Series: Hinsdale 1
USGS 7.5 Series: Lake San Cristobal, Red Cloud Peak, Handies Peak

• • •

Following the Lake Fork of the Gunnison, this route passes through an expansive valley before it climbs on a narrow shelf road to Burrows Park, which is rimmed with magnificent peaks. Wildflower-covered American Basin is the final destination.

Access

From Lake City drive south on Hwy. 149 for 2.3 miles. At a junction turn right onto County Road 30 toward Lake San Cristobal. Follow this road for 6.5 miles as it winds around the lake, turns to dirt, and climbs up the valley. Park on the side road across from Williams Creek Campground.

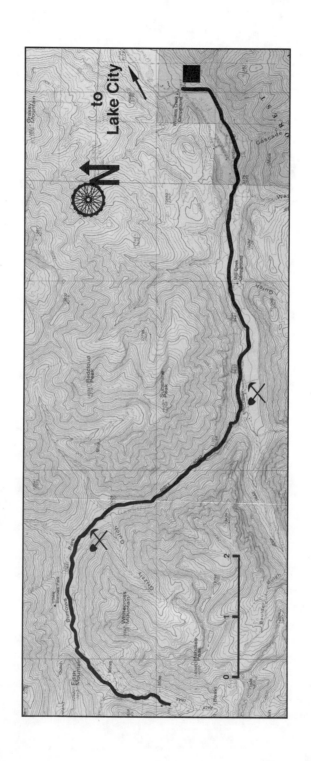

Description

Begin riding up the county road. At first it's wide and well maintained, making it a pleasant cruise. You pass ranches, small cabins, a campground, and several side roads. Towering mountains enclose this river land but the peaks at the head of the drainage seem to have a magnetic draw. The expanse of this valley comes to an abrupt end after about 5.3 miles of pedaling. You pass some old buildings and several beaver ponds before arriving at a junction. Two drainages tumble steeply to a confluence at this point. Easy pedaling ends here; the described route forks right and climbs to a shelf road leading to Cinnamon Pass. Before you continue this direction, take the left fork for a quick side trip to Sherman. The townsite is identified by a sign on the right of the road. A couple of old cabins are easy to spot; look more carefully and you'll see a few other foundations back in the trees. Ride a short distance farther to the stone base of a mill on the right. Novice riders planning to stop here may want to continue up the road to a peaceful lunch spot along Cottonwood Creek.

From the junction you begin climbing to the shelf road. Actually, a strong novice rider could pedal this section. It's not at all technical and the gradient remains moderate. The shelf road, carved into cliffs above the creek, is fairly level. There are plenty of places to pull over and peer down into the deep chasm below. Look carefully for the remains of a flume that was built precariously along the mountainside. It provided water that powered the mill in Sherman.

After a couple miles you leave the shelf road behind and ride into Burrows Park. Miners took full advantage of this unique flat area nestled in between the mountains and built quite a few settlements along the meadow. Some buildings, which have been restored, are right along the road. Others, smaller and more dilapidated, are concealed by trees and bushes. Mining was done along the sides of this valley and tailings dumps mark some of these operations. Even more mines were located higher up on the peaks. The road bisects the middle of the park as it crosses streams, passes a couple newer residences, and then curves left at the upper end of the valley. It's important to stay on designated roads through the park. Several spurs lead to private property but are well marked to help avoid trespassing.

Beyond Burrows Park you climb again, this time over more difficult terrain. Steeper pitches and some rocky spots slow your pace. A large mine, high above the left side of the road, and remains of a cabin and boiler are the only signs of activity in this pine-covered drainage. At roughly 13 miles you reach the side road for American Basin. Cinnamon Pass Road (an advanced ride) forks to the right. FS Road 3314 forks left and leads into American Basin. Another mile of pedaling over rocky terrain and across a large creek brings you deep into the basin and to the boundary of a BLM wilderness study area. Bikes are not allowed beyond this point, which is fine because the terrain doesn't appear bikeable anyway. An ideal Colorado scene of rushing waterfalls, tundra-covered hillsides, and a wildflower-lined creek makes this a great spot to sit and take a long break. If you still have some energy, it's a quick hike up to Sloan Lake, tucked back around the corner of the basin. When descending from American Basin, look across to the highest wooded knoll near Cinnamon Pass Road. You'll see the wooden skeleton of the enormous Tobasco Mill. The long downhill cruise back to your vehicle is sure to bring a satisfied smile to your face.

History

It's tough to visualize, from the few bleak remains, that Sherman had a hotel, several stores, the usual saloons, and a sawmill. The big mine in the area was Black Wonder; its mill foundations lie just above town. This mill's power was provided by a flume that ran from a dam above town. Sherman's unfortunate location, at the confluence of two drainages, meant that spring runoffs continually battered the small community. However, the town always endured and rebuilt until it experienced almost total obliteration in a flood when the dam broke in the early 1900s. This was the final straw. Although no residents were injured (everyone was at a dance in Lake City), the town never really recovered.

Burrows Park was a logical building site for prospectors mining this high valley and its surrounding peaks. Several camps were established including Tellurium, Argentum, Burrows Park, and Whitecross. Some confusion surrounds the exact location of the first three since some were basically summer tent camps. Tellurium may have been located across from the mine and boiler above the upper end of the park. It's short life makes any history difficult to trace. Whitecross was located just beyond the park between Tellurium and the flatter areas that supported Argentum. Many Whitecross residents worked at the nearby Tobasco Mill. Burrows Park might have actually been Argentum or the two may have eventually combined. At any rate, when all of these towns were established and full of excited miners this mountain valley must have echoed with activity.

Comments

The lower part of this road loses snow quite early and can be ridden in May. However, the road into American Basin usually doesn't open until late June. This ride can be easily shortened. A good place to park if you have less time is the junction near the Sherman townsite. During the off season, once traffic diminishes, the first few miles of this route would be a good family ride. Be alert for weather changes while in American Basin. It is above timberline and provides little shelter. Expect traffic on the lower section of road, though it diminishes somewhat at the junction near the shelf road. American Basin is usually deserted.

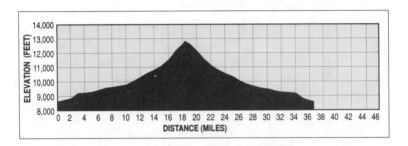

ENGINEER PASS

25

The first 9 miles up to Capitol City are easy riding.

Location: Lake City
Distance: 36.5 miles
Time: 6–7 hours
Rating: Easy*–more difficult
Low Elevation: 8,600 feet
High Point: 12,800 feet
Elevation Gain: 4,200 feet
Type: Out and back; dirt road
Season: May–October

Maps
Trails Illustrated: none for this
    region
USFS: Gunnison
USGS County Series: Hinsdale 1
USGS 7.5 Series: Lake City,
    Uncompahgre Peak, Red Cloud
    Peak, Handies Peak

• • •

The ride up one of Colorado's most famous passes starts on the temperate, cottonwood-lined streets of Lake City and climbs through tundra-covered hillsides to 12,800-foot Engineer Pass. This historic byway passes several townsites, aging mines, and mills before bringing riders to the San Juan high country.

Ride **25**   ENGINEER PASS

Access

In Lake City turn west onto Second Street at signs for the Scenic Byway/ Alpine Loop. Turn right at the stop sign and drive about a block. Park at the city park.

Description

Don't let the elevation gain and mileage discourage you; much of this route is easy. Even the final climb to Engineer Pass is completely rideable thanks to an excellent road surface. From the park, pedal back onto Second Street and turn right. Ride toward the steep gray walls of Henson Creek Canyon and follow the road up along the right side of the stream. After a couple miles of pedaling you climb above the creek, which disappears from sight into a deep gorge. Beyond a couple hills that give your lungs their first workout of the day, you ride through the Ute-Ulay mining complex and the townsite of Henson. Farther up the road at about 5.2 miles you pass Nellie Creek trailhead, climb several small hills, and pass more mining remains.

A major three-way junction at roughly 9 miles marks the end of the easy pedaling. Take a left here and pass the two remaining buildings of Capitol City. Climb moderately through an aspen grove and past Whitmore Falls. The peaks close in as you gain elevation more steadily, yet the gradient remains moderate and extremely bikeable. The valley narrows and silvery waterfalls stream out of steep side drainages. After nearly 13.5 miles you pass the hulking Red Rover Mill, which clings to a rock-strewn slope above the road.

Less than a mile farther up the road is a fork to the left for Rose's Cabin. It takes only a few minutes of pedaling up this fork to reach the site. Back on the main road you start some more difficult climbs. Rocks and steeper pitches become the norm but they're tempered by level recovery areas. Near timberline the road swings left and crosses a bridge. Above this point it begins to switchback for a final 2.5-mile ascent to the pass. The views north to the tundra expanse of American Flats and beyond to Big Blue Wilderness are worth a few minutes of contemplation. A couple of "fourteeners" grace this range, including 14,309-foot Uncompahgre Peak, the highest peak in the San Juans. It was first climbed in 1881 by Lake City residents. Several mines sit along the road, the highest being the Frank Hough, which lies just below the pass.

A wonderful feeling of accomplishment comes from reaching Engineer Pass under your own power, and on a mountain bike! Some jokester has scratched out the last zero on the pass sign, and your souvenir photos will slightly downplay the experience when they reveal your climb to a mere 1,280 feet. The road continues down to a junction where you can ride to either Silverton or Ouray, but don't attempt this unless you're prepared for an overnight situation. The return trip is one long, glorious downhill. Be careful of traffic and yield to vehicles on the narrower sections of road.

History

The heavily mined Henson Creek drainage provided the Lake City area with a long period of successful ore production. The Ute-Ulay mining complex began with initial discoveries in 1871. However, mining operations were delayed until the Ute Indians relinquished this land to the U.S. government. A busy operation, it contained a tram, a smelter, a processing mill, and a dam that provided water for a hydroelectric generating plant. One of the larger mines in the San Juans, the Ute-Ulay complex consistently produced rich amounts of galena, silver, lead, and gold. This promising record persuaded the Denver and Rio Grande Railroad to build a spur to the mine that ran until 1937. Henson, the surrounding community, housed the majority of the men working in nearby mines.

George T. Lee, who helped establish Capitol City, had high hopes for his meadow community. He predicted the town would surpass Denver in stature and become the state's new capital. In anticipation he built a beautiful brick "governor's mansion." His dream never materialized but the luxurious home provided an excellent site for his lavish parties. It was located at the lower end of the valley, but the house no longer exists. It was bulldozed in the early 1960s when the structure became unstable and dangerous. High ambitions also affected the planners of Capitol City and this small meadow was stuffed with an abundance of buildings including a $1,500 school built in 1883. Smelters were constructed on both sides of town. The brick smokestack of the upper one can still be seen over a mile up the road from Capitol City.

Structures at the Rose's Cabin site had a long and busy life. The original cabin was one of the first buildings constructed in the Lake City area. A man named Corydon Rose ran a hotel and bar. As the area filled with miners, more cabins sprang up, the site became an important stage stop, and a post office and stables were added to the settlement. Some of the buildings were remodeled in 1920 and modern plumbing was even installed. All that remains today are two foundations, the larger being that of a stable.

In the basin just below Engineer Pass sat the small summer community of Engineer City. Men from this mainly tent city worked at the Frank Hough Mine, which was discovered in 1882, as well as at other mines located on nearby Engineer Mountain. The town boasted (for a short time) of being the largest city in the state without a saloon. Supposedly the prospectors were too busy locating silver lodes. No matter how promising the ore appeared, mining proved to be too challenging a task at this elevation and the operations in this windswept basin never stayed open for long.

Comments

This ride is part of the Alpine Loop, a newly inaugurated backcountry route. Expect four-wheel-drive traffic but don't let it deter you from trying this ride. The lower part of the road has a longer riding season that starts in May and goes through October. Engineer Pass usually isn't open until July. Mileage can be shortened by parking farther up the road in one of many pullouts. An early start is a must for this ride. It's nice to be hours ahead of any potentially threatening weather so you can spend some time relaxing on the pass.

Rides Around Silverton–Ouray

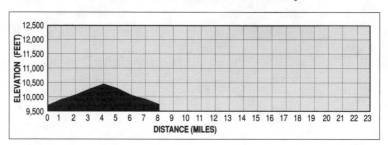

CUNNINGHAM GULCH

26

*This road has a few short, moderate climbs but because of the minimal mileage it can be completed by a novice.

Location: About 4 miles northeast of Silverton
Distance: 8 miles
Time: 2 hours
Rating: Easy*–moderate
Low Elevation: 9,680 feet
High Point: 10,480 feet
Elevation Gain: 800 feet
Type: Out and back; dirt road
Season: Late May–October

Maps
Trails Illustrated: none for this region
USFS: Uncompahgre
USGS County Series: San Juan
USGS 7.5 Series: Howardsville

• • •

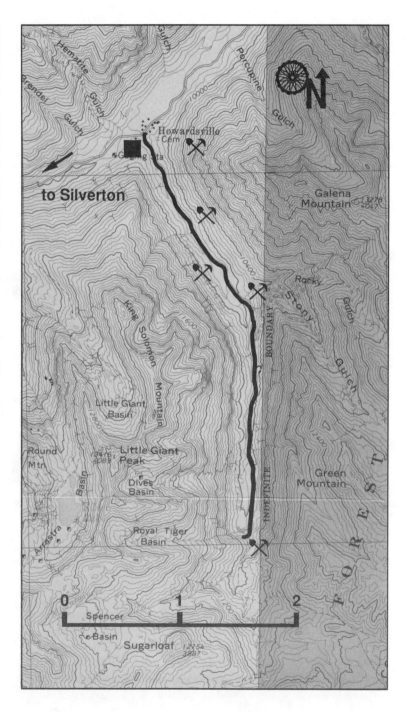

An easy climb through Cunningham Gulch passes mines, boarding houses, and aerial trams that are scattered along the road and perched on cliffs and crevices of the rock monoliths lining this valley.

Access

Drive through Silverton and turn right at the outskirts of town onto County Road 110 (marked by "Scenic Byway" signs). Follow this road for roughly 4 miles as it travels up the valley, turns to dirt, and passes a working mine. Turn right at the sign for Stony Pass and park right away on the wide spots off either side of the road. You've missed the turnoff if you go through a modern mining complex.

Description

Many of the historic remains in this gulch sit high on steep cliffs towering above this valley. There are some beautifully preserved buildings, especially on the left. Be prepared to ride with your head craned upward or stop a lot to search for the structures. Begin pedaling up this drainage, one of the most gradual in this area of the San Juan Mountains. The first mile is easy pedaling, which allows you the luxury of taking your eyes off the road for some history hunting. Bubbling Cunningham Creek is on your right for the entire ride. Soon you pass concrete foundations marking the newer of two mills built on this site for the Old Hundred Mine. Look to your left up Galena Mountain and you'll see remains of the Veta Madre Mine. Squint even harder and scan farther up to see the Old Hundred tram terminal and boarding house against the mountainside. (If you have a tough time spotting this, pedal a bit farther up the road and then try again.) The boarding house porch must have been a great place to drink a cup of coffee between mining stints but a terrible location to sit out a storm.

Beyond the Old Hundred site you climb some moderately steep hills but they don't last long. At about 1.2 miles the deteriorating remains of the Green Mountain Mill sit below the road. A huge multistory tramhouse, now a private residence, graces a left curve in the road. The Buffalo Boy tram still has buckets attached and you can follow the cable to higher towers standing near the top of Canby Mountain. After almost 1.7 miles of pedaling you pass a jeep road forking left for Stony Pass. A climb that starts out gradually but becomes very steep, this should only be attempted by advanced bikers. For this ride continue straight on the main road, which winds upward, leaving Cunningham Creek. A longer, moderate climb takes you higher above the creek. The road then levels out as you meet again with the bottom of the drainage. Many more mining remains dot the edges of the road and the hillsides above. On both sides of the creek you'll notice several avalanche paths. The steep sides of Cunningham Gulch create ideal routes for snowslides, and mines in this area were in continual danger of destruction from the powerful slides.

At approximately 4 miles you reach the head of the gulch. The road actually crosses the creek below foundations of the Highland Mary Mill and continues climbing. But it is no longer an easy ride and doesn't remain a road for much longer. You might want to drop your bike and hike up the road. It takes you to a trail that climbs to the edge of the Weminuche Wilderness Area and Highland Mary Lakes.

History

The original route of prospectors exploring the Animas Valley was from Del Norte over 12,588-foot Stony Pass and into Cunningham Gulch. This arduous path was the gateway into Silverton for many years. The route was initially a trail, and it took two weeks just to haul machinery for Silverton's first sawmill over the path. In 1879 the route was enlarged into a wagon road, making it easier for fortune seekers to swarm into the area. Machinery for the first mill in the region was hauled over this road by wagon. Once railroads were brought into the valley traffic over Stony Pass diminished and the route fell into disrepair. An ambitious plan to drive the first automobile into Silverton via Stony Pass in 1910 meant major repairs to the road. The car made it but had to be hauled up steeper sections by a team of horses.

Barely visible among the modern buildings of the mining operation at the mouth of the gulch are a few remains of Howardsville. This town developed as a result of traffic that poured out of the gulch and into the valley when Stony Pass was used. Howardsville became the county seat (it was the first county seat in western Colorado) in 1874 but held the honored position for only a year, after which the position was moved to Silverton. The settlement thrived even after a decline in traffic over Stony Pass. Construction of the railroad from Silverton to Animas Forks helped development of mines around Howardsville and ensured its existence, at least for a time. Finally the lure of an increasingly active Silverton caused many residents to leave Howardsville.

Several successful mines operated along the sides of Cunningham Gulch. The Old Hundred Mining Company owned 30 claims on Galena Mountain. Seven large veins crisscrossed Galena's slopes and all contained great amounts of valuable ore. The Green Mountain Mill, which received frequent batterings by snowslides, was built in the early 1900s. A branch of the Silverton Northern Railroad was extended to this site in 1904 to transport ore to nearby smelters. Buffalo Boy Mine, discovered in 1883, operated periodically until 1925. It was then purchased by a mining company, which erected the 8,740-foot tram. A fire destroyed the lower tram building in 1935. It was rebuilt, but a second fire in 1936 destroyed other buildings just after the lower tramhouse was finished, causing the company to lose interest in the operation. The small community of Niegoldtown developed near Buffalo Boy tram. A center of activity at the base of Stony Pass, it remained a small camp since most travelers continued on to more active Howardsville. Highland Mary Mine is surrounded by a fascinating story. The original owner, Edward Ennis, arrived in the area after receiving directions from a spiritualist on where to locate a lake of silver. This same spiritualist guided Ennis to a site suitable for digging a tunnel. Although short on money in later years, Ennis hung on to his mine, refusing to sell without permission from the spiritualist. He died an insane man. Another company eventually bought the mine and worked it off and on until 1952, when the mill burned down.

Comments

This is a good ride if you don't have a lot of time. It can also be extended into a full day exploration by choosing the hiking option where the described ride ends.

Elegant remains of the Animas Forks townsite are located in the mountains northeast of Silverton (ride 27).

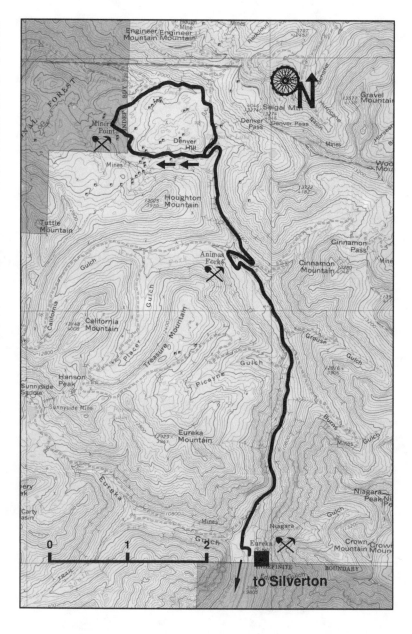

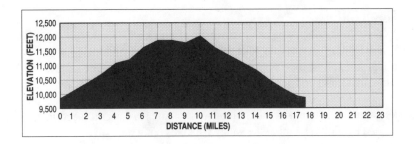

MINERAL POINT

27

A physically fit novice could bike as far as Animas Forks. The road is rough but climbs gradually.

Location: About 7.5 miles northeast of Silverton
Distance: 17.5 miles
Time: 5 hours
Rating: Moderate*–more difficult
Low Elevation: 9,840 feet
High Point: 12,000 feet
Elevation Gain: 2,160 feet
Type: Out and back, loop; dirt road
Season: Late June–early October

Maps
Trails Illustrated: none for this region
USFS: Uncompahgre
USGS County Series: San Juan
USGS 7.5 Series: Handies Peak

• • •

The Mineral Point ride travels among huge rust-colored mountains, providing an excellent overview of the mineral-rich area around Silverton. Mines, mills, and ghost towns tumble out of side canyons and dot many mountainsides.

Access
Drive through Silverton and turn right at the outskirts of town onto County Road 110 (marked by "Scenic Byway" signs). Follow this road for roughly 7.5 miles as it travels up the valley, turns to dirt, and passes a couple working mines. Park off the right of the road just before a bridge.

Description

Your starting point is the empty townsite of Eureka. Concrete foundations from the huge Sunnyside Mill tumble down a nearby hillside. Cross a bridge and follow the road that climbs along the left side of the valley. The canyon narrows and you gain elevation quickly as the road rises above the Animas River. You're on the bed of the Silverton Northern Railroad and its gradual grade makes the frequent rocky patches easier to negotiate.

At a little over 3 miles the valley widens, giving the road more room to meander. It crosses the river and resumes climbing, now along the right side of the drainage. The buildings of Animas Forks appear in the distance. Pass a fork to the right for Cinnamon Pass at about 3.7 miles. Continue straight and head up the valley toward Animas Forks. Cross the river again and climb a rough section of road into town. Many well-preserved buildings sit between the two forks of the Animas River. They suffer a lot of wear and tear from curious history buffs. Help preserve these beautiful structures by observing them from a distance.

Beyond Animas Forks the ride changes to a more difficult rating as it leaves the railroad grade and follows a four-wheel-drive road. Drop down to a three-way intersection on the upper edge of town. The left fork climbs into California Gulch, another bikeable route. Take the right fork, which crosses the river and climbs to a switchback at another three-way junction marked by a sign for Cinnamon and Engineer Passes. Turn left and follow the road, which becomes much more narrow and rocky (but is still completely rideable) as it begins a long, moderate climb along the drainage. You quickly reach timberline and have a bird's-eye view of the enormous Bagley Mill near the mouth of California Gulch.

Pass another fork to the right for Cinnamon Pass and head toward the prominent knob of Denver Hill. Veer to the left, leave the river, and climb to a three-way junction at roughly 6.7 miles. Take the left fork toward Mineral Point. You're on the beginning of the loop that circles the basin below Denver Hill. The undulating road travels over smooth and rocky terrain, passing mining remains that clutter the basin and spill out of side gulches. Not too many vehicles explore this high alpine park and you may have it to yourself. Hang right at a junction near a rusted boiler. Drop into a meadow and skirt a jeep-sucking bog. On a bike the bog is easy to avoid by staying on high ground to the left. Beyond the bog you cross a stream, pass a fork to the left, and cross another stream. The camp of Mineral Point once lay in this area.

A junction appears shortly after the second stream crossing. Take the left fork and descend a short distance over steep terrain to the crumbling San Juan Chief Mill. Avoid the maze of roads around the mill by staying to the right of, and above, the buildings. Climb a couple of short, steep, technical pitches and pass a fork to the right. Cross a small creek and ride to a four-way intersection. Continue straight and merge almost immediately with Engineer Pass Road. Turn right, climb to a high point, and descend toward the Animas River drainage. Pass a fork to the left for Engineer Pass and curve to the right around Denver Hill. You'll come to the junction where the loop started. Turn left and backtrack past Animas Forks and to your vehicle.

History

Eureka was the probable site of this area's first gold discovery during 1861. The mainstay of this community was the Sunnyside Mine, which eventually became the best producer in the region. Discovered in 1873, the mine was located 2,000 feet above town in Eureka Gulch. The mill, built in 1899, was connected to the mine by a three-mile-long tram. After the mine discontinued operations in the 1930s, the mill was dismantled and sold for $225,000. As the Sunnyside Mine prospered, population soared in Eureka. During its peak years the town had about 2,000 residents. There's been a lot of speculation about the tall skeletal remains of a building in the meadow, my favorite theory being that fire hoses were hung out to dry there.

During 1875 the famous road builder Otto Mears constructed a toll road up the Animas Valley to Mineral Point. In 1904 the Silverton Northern narrow gauge line was extended to Animas Forks and used this toll road for its route. This section of the railway was only open until 1916 but during its brief existence offered stylish meals including a wine list in the dining car. Service continued as far as Eureka until 1939.

Animas Forks was established in 1877. People were enticed to its isolated mountain location by offers of free lots and assistance in building their homes. The town prospered during the late 1870s and 1880s. A telephone line was even brought in from Lake City. Foundations of the gargantuan 100-stamp Gold Prince Mill can be seen near the river below town. After operating for only a few years this mill was dismantled and hauled down for use at Eureka. Many fascinating residences are still standing. The elegant house with the bay window was rumored to be the home of Thomas Walsh, owner of the massive Camp Bird Mine near Ouray. The small square structure sitting alone on the lower edge of town was the jail.

The land around Mineral Point was worked thoroughly for valuable ore but an inhospitable environment kept the area from ever developing into a successful community. For a while the town, which contained a post office, stores, saloons, a sawmill, and cabins, prospered with populations reaching 1,000. Its decline began in the late 1880s, due in part to large amounts of false advertising. Investors were lured to the area by pictures of steamboats on the river and trolley cars on the road, and more than one left disappointed after sinking money into shafts that produced nothing. The San Juan Chief Mill never amounted to much and was shut down when it was still new because of the rapid decline in silver values in 1893.

Comments

As with all heavily mined areas it is important to stay on designated roads and away from the many mining structures along this route. Above Animas Forks you're in incredibly exposed terrain and should plan accordingly regarding the weather. This area has always been popular with four-wheelers, and you will have to share the road with others.

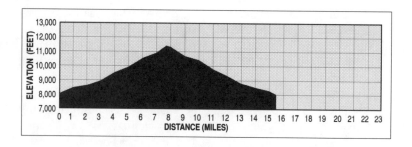

YANKEE BOY BASIN

28

Location: Ouray
Distance: 15.5 miles
Time: 4–5 hours
Rating: More difficult–advanced
Low Elevation: 8,000 feet
High Point: 11,440 feet
Elevation Gain: 3,440 feet
Type: Out and back; dirt road
Season: Late June–early October

Maps
Trails Illustrated: none for this
    region
USFS: Uncompahgre
USGS County Series: Ouray 2
USGS 7.5 Series: Ouray, Ironton,
    Telluride

• • •

Ride **28** YANKEE BOY BASIN

High alpine waterfalls and a wildflower paradise greet bikers who tackle the climb into Yankee Boy Basin. The high peaks surrounding this protected valley harbor valuable minerals, and this route passes many of the mines built to extract this wealth.

Access

From Ouray take Hwy. 550 south toward Silverton. Drive about 0.5 miles and turn right onto County Road 361 at the sign for Box Canyon Falls. Drive a short distance up this road and cross over a bridge. Park at a pullout on the left side of the road just after the bridge.

Description

This road is well maintained for the first few miles but gains a lot of elevation. It starts out immediately with a steep climb that's sure to wake up those sleepy muscles. Above this stretch the grade backs off a bit, becoming less strenuous. There's even some downhill before you cross a bridge and start another climb. You ride over a short section of pavement and continue a steep ascent. This narrow road is squeezed in between sheer rock walls that rise on one side of the road and drop straight down on the other. Numerous pullouts give you plenty of chances to rest and gaze at the glistening gray cliffs of this awesome canyon. Be sure to give vehicles ample room to pass on the shelf-like sections of road.

Soon it's switchback time and you gain a lot of elevation in a hurry. Beyond the switchbacks muster your energy for an extended haul over another steep grade. After almost 4.4 miles of pedaling you pass the huge mining complex of Camp Bird. At a junction take the right fork and continue to climb along the side of the canyon. Ride under Hanging Rock, a cliff overhang that must have been created by some dynamite experts. The road, hemmed in by the steep walls of this narrow valley, begins to climb up Sneffels Creek drainage. Whenever you pull over to rest, look upward in search of mining remains, which cling precariously to mountainside ledges.

At a little over 5.7 miles you pass a fork on the left for Imogene Pass. This incredibly challenging route sees a lot of mountain-bike traffic. Continue straight and pedal a short distance farther to the Sneffels townsite. The nearby Revenue Mine, displaying some modern structures, has operated sporadically in recent years. Beyond this point the road smooths out for a while and passes the crumbling remains of the immense Atlas Mill, above the left side of the creek.

At a junction beyond the mill take the right fork toward Yankee Boy Basin. The left fork leads to Governor Basin and as you climb above the junction you can peek into this area and see well-preserved mining structures that have managed to survive in exposed locations. Beyond the junction the road becomes much rougher and more of a typical jeep road. You'll have to pick your way among the rocks but overall the route is very rideable. Twin waterfalls tumbling over ledges alongside the road might look familiar — they appeared in Coors beer commercials. A vast array of wildflowers carpets the upper part of this basin, with July being the best viewing time. Several side roads branch off the main route, which remains obvious. It curves to the left toward the head of the basin near the tailings and few remaining timbers of the Yankee Boy Mine. A short distance beyond the mine the road begins a long climb up a grassy slope to Wright's Lake.

I decided to end the ride at the foot of this climb and took a spur road into the basin for a well-earned lunch break. You can bike (be prepared for a workout) or hike this last mile of road to the lake. Beyond that point it degenerates into a trail and enters wilderness area. The descent from this basin is special, not only because you're going downhill, but also because of the completely different perspective you get of the mountains. They appear almost larger than they did when you were going up. Be exceptionally cautious when you descend along the dropoffs. Pull off for vehicles, allowing enough room both for them and for you.

History

It was a struggle to build a road to Camp Bird and four attempts were made before the road and railroad engineer Otto Mears succeeded in 1881. During the peak mining years this route was lined with wagons, mule trains, and pack burros moving ore and supplies 24 hours a day. The story of Camp Bird Mine is basically the story of Thomas Walsh, who discovered high-grade gold ore in the area. He bought up most of the claims in Imogene Basin and developed Camp Bird Mine, which produced over $26 million between 1896 and 1910. The mine was high above the mill and a 9,000-foot long tramway connected the two. Thomas Walsh sold the mine in 1902 to an English company for $5 million. He moved to Washington, D.C., and adopted an extravagant lifestyle. His daughter became known for her lavish tastes and for a time owned the Hope Diamond. The current mill that you see from the road was built in 1960. Camp Bird Mine continues to operate sporadically but was shut down when I was there in August 1990.

Sneffels was started earlier than Camp Bird and grew as the Revenue Mine developed. During its heyday between 1881 and 1919 the population was around 300, although it dropped much lower in the winter. Revenue Mine was actually an offshoot of the Virginius, which was located high above Sneffels in Humboldt Basin. The struggle of operating a mine at such high elevations led to the boring of Revenue Tunnel. It went 7,800 feet into the mountain and intersected the lower workings of the Virginius operation 2,000 feet below the latter's original shaft. Ore was dropped down through the tunnel and exited out a portal near the mill, simplifying the arduous process of hauling ore down the mountain. These mines contained both gold and silver ore and after the silver market crashed the gold veins were exploited. During their boom days between 1882 and 1911, 50 miles of tunnel on the Revenue-Virginius property produced about $27 million of ore. The operation closed down in the early 1900s. A huge mill that once stood where a smaller, more modern building sits today was destroyed by fire in the 1920s. The population of Sneffels dropped and the post office closed in 1930.

Comments

Rotten weather can move into this area with frightening speed. The upper edge of the basin is just above timberline, so you can get down into trees quickly but you still don't want to be caught up here during a bad storm. Expect traffic, because four-wheelers love this area. However, they're moving as slowly or slower than you are, which makes the situation easier to deal with. Besides, the scenery and historic nature of this ride seem to make it easier to share the road with others.

The route into Yankee Boy Basin clings to steep cliffs above Canyon Creek.

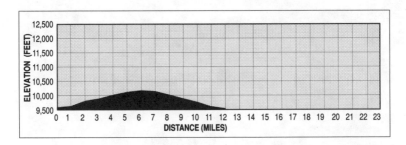

LIZARD HEAD PASS

29

Location: About 11.6 miles south-west of Telluride
Distance: 12 miles
Time: 2–3 hours
Rating: Easy
Low Elevation: 9,520 feet
High Point: 10,250 feet
Elevation Gain: 730 feet
Type: Out and back; dirt road
Season: June–October

Maps
Trails Illustrated: none for this
    region
USFS: Uncompahgre
USGS County Series: San Miguel 3
USGS 7.5 Series: Mt. Wilson, Ophir

• • •

Lizard Head Pass, with its expansive meadows and stunning mountain views, is the destination of this easy cruise along a section of the Rio Grande Southern Railroad grade.

Access

From Telluride drive out to the three-way junction. Turn left onto Hwy. 145 toward Ophir, Rico, and Cortez. Drive 8.6 miles and park off the highway on the right on a section of old road just above a private drive, which leads to a mining site. This pullout is directly across the highway from a driveway and a couple old cabins. If you pass the campground sign you've gone too far.

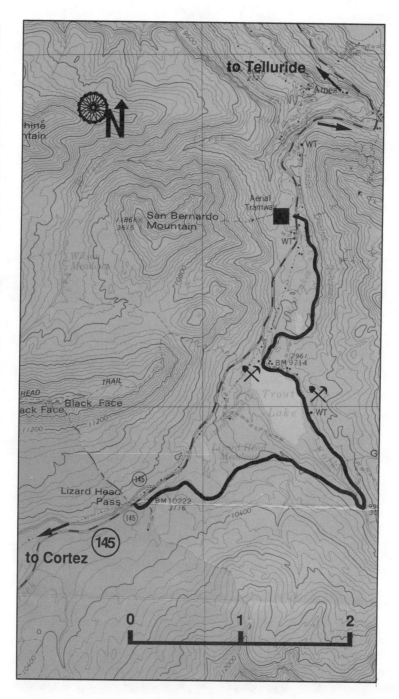

Description

Ride up the highway a very short distance and turn onto a road forking left in between a private driveway and the campground entrance. It passes a house on the right, crosses under the power lines, and disappears into the aspen. What was once the railroad grade is now a smooth dirt road that climbs above the campground and gradually works its way up the left side of the drainage toward Lizard Head Pass. After a little over a mile of riding you pass a fork to the right that drops to Priest Lake. The lake, nestled in a small basin, makes a pretty picture with the surrounding mountains as a backdrop. A couple of sturdily built cabins grace the lake's shoreline.

As you ride along the railroad grade look for the remains of an old flume above the left side of the road. Now almost entirely disintegrated, it carried water down the valley to the Ames power plant. At about 1.7 miles you come to a junction near the dam for Trout Lake. Turn left and follow the grade around the left side of the lake. Summer cottages dot the slopes of this small community. A restored storage tank, which provided water for the narrow gauge train, stands along the road near the far edge of the lake.

Beyond Trout Lake you cross over the Lake Fork of the San Miguel River just above an old trestle, one of the few still standing from the old railways of Colorado. After several more miles of gradual climbing through hillside forests and meadows you reach Lizard Head Pass. Large meadows open up on both sides of the saddle and close-up views of the Lizard Head rock formation dominate the skyline. The grade ends at a parking area near the highway. A dirt road curving left toward the edge of some trees leads to secluded lunch spots. A couple of interpretive signs on the other side of the highway near a trailhead highlight some of the historic features of this area. If you're interested in doing more exploring, hike along the trail that starts at the information board and accesses the Lizard Head Wilderness Area. From the pass, return as you came.

History

Lizard Head Pass saw very little use the first few years of Telluride's existence. The main route out of town climbed over the mountains toward Ouray and it wasn't until the train pushed its way toward Telluride that Lizard Head Pass become known and was approved as a workable mountain crossing for the railroad route to Durango. At 10,250 feet it was the highest point on the Rio Grande Southern line. Otto Mears, the "Pathfinder of the San Juans," put his skill as a designer of railroads to work and engineered the grade to Telluride and up over the pass to Durango. Construction of the 160-mile Rio Grande Southern line began in both Durango and Ridgeway in 1890. The narrow gauge line took 21 months to build, cost over $9 million dollars, and crossed over 130 bridges, the longest measuring 544 feet. Heavy demand the first few years kept 35 locomotives operating on this route. However, the crash of the silver market caused near abandonment of the line, with shipments of lumber and coal barely keeping it alive. In spite of many hardship situations, the railroad continued running until 1951. To cut expenses, the steam engines were replaced with an odd-looking contraption called the Galloping Goose. A Pierce Arrow automobile grafted to a truck bed and set on railroad wheels, this gasoline-powered conveyance carried both freight and passengers.

The water from Trout Lake was used to generate electricity by a small power plant at Ames that provided the first long-distance transmission of alternating electric current for industrial purposes. The recipient of this power was the Gold King Mine, located high on Silver Mountain above Ophir. In 1909, water from an exceptionally wet August and September overloaded Trout Lake and the dam burst. Over 16 miles of railroad track were taken out in the flood and Telluride became more isolated than it had been in 30 years. Until the track could be rebuilt the town resorted to bringing in supplies by mule and wagon. The first load to arrive brought only beer, kegs and kegs of it. Repairs to the line cost $134,000, a pittance these days but then an expensive blow to a barely surviving railway.

Comments

You may want to bring fishing gear on this ride and try your luck at Trout Lake.

Many standing structures still grace the hillsides of the Alta mining camp (ride 30).

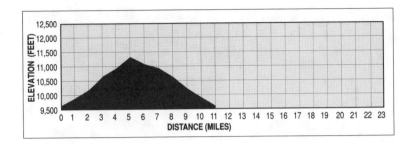

ALTA AND BEYOND

30

*A biker of moderate ability could ride to Alta. The loop beyond Alta has a more difficult rating.

Location: About 7.7 miles south-west of Telluride
Distance: 11 miles
Time: 3 hours
Rating: Moderate*–more difficult
Low Elevation: 9,600 feet
High Point: 11,280 feet
Elevation Gain: 1,680 feet
Type: Out and back, loop; dirt road
Season: June–October

Maps
Trails Illustrated: none for this
  region
USFS: Uncompahgre
USGS County Series: San Miguel 3
USGS 7.5 Series: Telluride, Ophir,
  Grayhead

• • •

A climb into the mountains south of Telluride takes you to the scenic town of Alta. Perched on a knoll, this well-preserved settlement has some of the best mountain views in the state. Optional side trips into nearby basins offer close-up peeks of the area's mines and high alpine lakes.

Access

From Telluride drive out to the three-way junction. Turn left onto Hwy. 145 toward Ophir, Rico, and Cortez. Drive about 4.8 miles, past the Sunshine Campground on the right. Just beyond the campground look for a dirt road forking left into the aspen. Pull onto this road and park at the wide areas on either side. Avoid blocking the road.

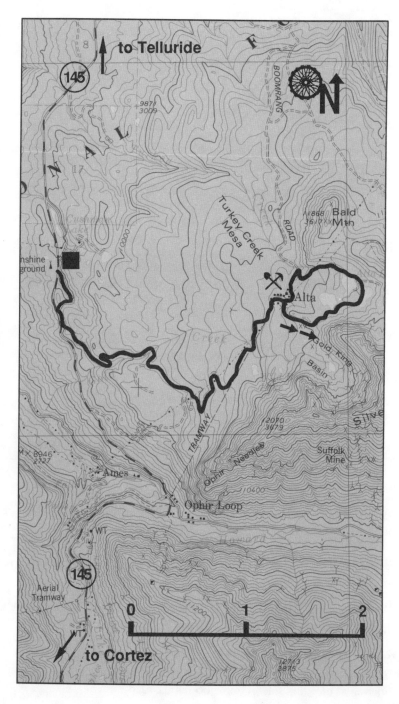

Description

Follow this dirt road a short distance. It drops you onto Alta Road just above its junction with the highway. Pedal along Alta Road as it starts climbing through a series of switchbacks. Although the grade never becomes overwhelmingly steep, you do get a workout. Expect some rocky sections, which are easy to weave around. A dense canopy of aspen and pine filters the sunlight, keeping the route shady and cool. After a couple of switchbacks look for the serrated Ophir Needles that create a formidable fence of rock to the southeast.

After about 1.9 miles of pedaling you pass a road forking left at the edge of a hillside meadow. Stay on the main road and pass another spur on the right a short distance later. The road continues gaining elevation as it switchbacks into an open area and then levels out a bit. Fat, sassy marmots were sunbathing on the rocks in this meadow the morning I rode past. You pass a couple side roads that lead to campsites before you ride back into the trees. At roughly 3.5 miles a well-traveled road forks to the left. It accesses an area currently being worked by a mining company and is marked with "No Trespassing" signs. The main road curves left here and begins the final climb to Alta.

You can't miss the town. Its tailings slopes, cabins, and impressive houses spill down the hillside to the road. You ride between several weathered buildings to a flat spot that's perfect for gawking at the million-dollar view across the valley. The prominent rock formation that stands isolated from the rest of the peaks is Lizard Head. I've spent a lot of time trying to see the reptilian features in this pinnacle and have never succeeded. Looking around Alta you'll notice several houses with much more durable construction, identifying this as a more recent ghost town. These dwellings are quite a contrast to the rustic log cabins that make up some of Colorado's ghost camps. A sturdily built boarding house stands across the road on the edge of the knoll. (I wonder if the owner charged extra for rooms with a view.)

Just below the boarding house is a three-way junction and a small sign for Alta Lakes. Turn right here onto a side road, cross a small stream, and curve around the right side of a hill. After a steep, half-mile climb you reach another junction. Follow the right fork for a short side trip into Gold King Basin, where the remains of the large Gold King mining operation sit.

Back on the main road, climb to the saddle just above the junction and descend to Alta Lakes. Since these lakes are popular with fishermen you may see quite a few people. At a junction near a Forest Service information board and just before the lake, turn right for a short loop ride around Alta Lakes. Pedal counterclockwise around the largest of the lakes and past a smaller one on the right. The road you're following dead ends at the far end of the lake, but across the creek you can turn right onto another road that climbs steeply over a small ridge and into a basin holding the third lake. This lake, the most beautiful and peaceful of the three, lies at the base of a steeply walled cirque. Numerous places to sit and marvel at the beauty of the area make this a good lunch spot. Follow a rough road that climbs and descends around the left side of the lake. It curves to the left, leading away from the lake and down a draw. You descend, sometimes steeply, over loose rock and under powerlines until the trail eventually merges with a much more distinct road. Turn left onto this road and ride a short distance up to Alta to complete the loop. From the town, return as you came.

History

Never an incorporated town, Alta was the company settlement for Gold King Mine. Although a fairly large community, it had no church or post office. Basically a one-mine settlement, it relied almost entirely on the success of the Gold King for its existence. This mine was discovered in the 1870s and produced gold, silver, lead, and copper. It had several spells of productivity and was worked off and on until 1945. The nearby Black Hawk tunnel supposedly reaches 9,000 feet back into the mountains to access rich veins that have produced between $15 and $20 million of valuable ore. Ore from the mines in Gold King Basin was transported to the three mills in Alta by aerial tram. All three mills, including a large 40-stamp structure, have burned down. Another 2-mile long tram brought ore to a railroad loading bin in the town of Ophir. This amazing system of cables and buckets ran from Alta along the edge of Ophir Needles before it dropped down onto what is now a large bend in the highway. The Gold King was the first mine in the country to have electricity to run its machinery. A small power plant, located below Ophir at Ames, provided the power.

Comments

Although the first 4 miles gain quite a bit of elevation they can be ridden by a biker with moderate ability because of their nontechnical nature. Alta's buildings seem sturdy, but they've been standing a long time and are best protected by being observed from a distance. Both fishermen and history buffs travel this road, so expect some traffic.

ADDITIONAL RIDES IN REGION 4
• • •

Spring Creek Pass
Following a rarely used jeep road that is part of the Colorado Trail, this ride is almost entirely above timberline and has unsurpassed views of numerous mountain ranges. Marked as FS Road 550, the route begins at the picnic area on Spring Creek Pass, located about 15 miles southeast of Lake City on Hwy. 149. A 16-mile out and back ride, it climbs and descends moderately through trees and over alpine tundra to a saddle between two knolls, one of which is marked by a small communications tower. The route actually continues, but it turns into a trail more suitable for hiking.

Alpine Plateau
The Alpine Plateau provides an ideal change of pace from Lake City's steep terrain. Approach this high, flat mesa by driving 11 miles north of Lake City on Hwy. 149 and then following the Alpine Plateau Road for 5 miles to Soldier Summit. Park here and ride up FS Road 867 to the plateau. The fairly level road winds in and out of forested areas and meadows, offering many views back toward peaks in the Big Blue Wilderness. Watch for a fork on the right after the mile 10 marker. Follow this side road across a large meadow and over some bumpy sections for about a mile to reach a knoll where the road begins to descend. Expansive views to the north and east make this a good place to eat lunch before you turn around. Even novice riders could pedal this 11-mile out and back ride.

Lime Creek Road
Traveling a secluded drainage, Lime Creek Road follows part of the original road from Durango to Silverton. Lined almost entirely with aspen, this route is enhanced by views into the West Needle Mountains. The road can be reached from Silverton by following Hwy. 550 over Molas Pass and descending 4 miles to the upper end or 12 miles to the lower end. Of the several ways to ride Lime Creek, the most decadent is to start at the upper end and have a car waiting at the finish. This makes the majority of this 12-mile long road a descent. Another possibility is to ride from the lower end and go as far as you want. One good destination is lily pad-filled Scout

Lake. Both of these options are rated moderate. A third choice, which requires some physical endurance, is to ride up the highway and loop back on Lime Creek Road.

Little Molas Lake

This ride follows an absolutely exquisite 8-mile section of the Colorado Trail. Easily accessed from Silverton by following Hwy. 550 up to Molas Pass, the trail starts at Little Molas Lake. Identified by Colorado Trail markers, the route alternates between single track and old road for 2 miles and then follows a contouring single track along slopes topped by impressive cliffs. It meanders in and out of drainages, past beautiful meadows, and through brilliant fields of wildflowers. The first few miles could be pedaled by a moderate rider while the final 3-mile climb requires more advanced technical skills. The trail continues all the way to Durango; however, those riding just for the day may want to turn around at the saddle marked by a large *cairn.*

River Road

The old railroad grade from Ouray to Ridgway is an easy ride that parallels the Uncompahgre River and passes scenic ranches. If you plan just right, you could ride the 11 miles and arrive in the quaint town of Ridgway in time for lunch. To access River Road from the main street of Ouray turn onto 7th Street, descend to the river, cross a bridge, and turn right onto the railroad grade. After riding through the outskirts of town, you descend gradually around a small lake and pass some homes before you drop into lush green pastures. The road makes a sharp left, climbs a small hill, and turns sharply right before the final coast into Ridgway. The return trip is enhanced by the scenic transition from pastures to soaring peaks.

Sneffels Vista

The foothills north of Sneffels Wilderness Area contain moderate terrain near one of Colorado's most scenic mountain ranges. To reach this area turn onto County Road 5 (marked by a sign for the Girl Scout camp) in the small town of Ridgway, located about 11 miles north of Ouray. Follow this road for roughly 5 miles and park at a three-way junction near a cattle guard. Cross the cattle guard and climb along a National Forest access road through meadows bordered by scrub oak and into dense groves of aspen. Avoid any side roads: they lead to private property. Beyond the National Forest boundary the road climbs into forests alternating between pine and aspen. After approximately 5 miles of pedaling you reach a steep hillside meadow where the riding becomes much more strenuous. This is a good place to turn around.

Ilium Valley

The glaciated Ilium Valley has some of the flatter pedaling terrain around Telluride. This area can be accessed from two locations. Intermediate riders can take a single-track section of the railroad grade that starts from the highway junction 3 miles west of Telluride, descends along the San Miguel River, and merges with Ilium Road. If you follow the single track be aware that you are on private land and need to stay on the railroad grade. Novices can drive about 5.4 miles down the valley from town to the beginning of Ilium Road. Once in the valley you have several options. You can cruise along the well-maintained Ilium Road. Or, you can cross the river at Camp Ilium and follow roads forking both left and right from the hill on the other side of the bridge. Both these routes eventually dead end but are worth exploring.

Last Dollar Loop

Telluride is famous for its mountains and broad mesas. The Last Dollar ride incorporates the terrain of both in a 25-mile, moderate–more difficult loop. It begins 11 miles down the valley in Sawpit. Start riding back up the highway and get on County Road M59, which is dirt and winds along the river for about 4 miles. After you rejoin the highway, descend a few feet and turn right onto FS Road 639. Climb up along Deep Creek to connect with Last Dollar Road. Turn left and follow this road as it meanders along the mesa and then climbs steeply to a saddle. After a speedy descent into expansive ranch lands, fork left onto County Road 58P. Follow this road through more open meadows and back down to Sawpit.

Bikeable Passes

Region 4 contains some of the highest passes in Colorado. Several of these are bikeable, including Engineer, Cinnamon, Stony, Black Bear, Ophir, and Imogene. A multiday credit card loop, in which you stay in a different town every night, is possible using some of these passes.

APPENDIX

Rides By Difficulty

Easy

Gold Camp Road, p. 2
Cripple Creek, p. 6

Lizard Head Pass, p. 143

Easy–moderate

Argentine Central Railroad Grade,
   p. 11
Alma Loop, p. 52
Leadville Loop, p. 62

Chalk Creek, p. 66
Gold Creek, p. 81
Poverty Gulch, p. 99
Cunningham Gulch, p. 129

Easy–more difficult

Cumberland Pass Loop, p. 85
Pieplant, p. 89

American Basin, p. 121
Engineer Pass, p. 125

Easy–advanced

Alpine Tunnel, p. 71

Moderate

Cemetery Loop, p. 16

Oh-My-God Road, p. 21

Moderate–more difficult

Peru Creek, p. 39
Golden Horseshoe, p. 43
Sacramento, p. 57
Paradise Divide, p. 103

Ruby, p. 107
Lead King Basin, p. 111
Mineral Point, p. 134
Alta and Beyond, p. 147

More difficult

Kingston Peak, p. 26

More difficult–advanced

Yankee Boy Basin, p. 138

Advanced

St. Mary's Glacier Loop, p. 30
Montezuma Loop, p. 48

Canyon Creek, p. 94

Suggested Contacts

Front Range

Boulder Ranger District
(Central City)
2995 Baseline Rd., Rm. 110
Boulder, CO 80303
(303) 444-6001

Central City Public Relations
P.O. Box 249
Central City, CO 80427
(303) 573-0247

Clear Creek Ranger District
(Georgetown, Idaho Springs,
Central City)
P.O. Box 3307
Idaho Springs, CO 80452
(303) 567-2901

Georgetown Chamber of Commerce
P.O. Box 444
Georgetown, CO 80444
(303) 569-2888

Idaho Springs Information Center
P.O. Box 97
Idaho Springs, CO 80452
(303) 567-4382

Pikes Peak Ranger District
(Cripple Creek)
601 S. Weber St.
Colorado Springs, CO 80903
(719) 636-1602

The Crucible (Cripple Creek)
P.O. Box 650
Cripple Creek, CO 80813
(719) 689-2307

East Central

Dillon Ranger District
(Summit County)
P.O. Box 620
Silverthorne, CO 80498
(303) 468-5400

Summit County Chamber of
Commerce
P.O. Box 214
Frisco, CO 80443
(303) 668-5800

South Park Ranger District
(Fairplay)
P.O. Box 219
Fairplay, CO 80440
(719) 836-2031

Park County Tourism Office
(Fairplay)
P.O. Box 701
Fairplay, CO 80440
(719) 836-2771

East Central

Leadville Ranger District
2015 N. Poplar
Leadville, CO 80461
(719) 486-0752

Leadville Chamber of Commerce
P.O. Box 861
Leadville, CO 80461
(719) 486-3900

Salida Ranger District
 (Buena Vista)
230 W. 16th
Salida, CO 81201
(719) 539-3591

Buena Vista Chamber of Commerce
P.O. Box 2021
Buena Vista, CO 81211
(719) 395-6612

West Central

Aspen Ranger District
806 W. Hallam
Aspen, CO 81611
(303) 925-3445

Sopris Ranger District (Aspen)
P.O. Box 309
Carbondale, CO 81623
(303) 963-2266

Aspen Visitor Center
303 E. Main St.
Aspen, CO 81611
(303) 925-1940

Taylor River/Cebolla Ranger
Districts (Crested Butte, Gunnison)
216 N. Colorado
Gunnison, CO 81230
(303) 641-0471

Crested Butte Chamber of Commerce
P.O. Box 1288
Crested Butte, CO 81224
(303) 349-6438

Gunnison Chamber of Commerce
P.O. Box 36
Gunnison, CO 81230
(303) 641-1501

San Juans

Animas Ranger District
(Silverton)
110 W. 11th St.
Durango, CO 81301
(303) 247-4874

Silverton Chamber of Commerce
P.O. Box 565
Silverton, CO 80433
(303) 387-5654

San Juans

Cebolla Ranger District (Lake City)
216 N. Colorado
Gunnison, CO 81230
(303) 641-0471

Ouray Chamber of Commerce
P.O. Box 145
Ouray, CO 81427
(303) 325-4747

Lake City Chamber of Commerce
P.O. Box 430
Lake City, CO 81235
(303) 944-2527

Norwood Ranger District (Telluride)
P.O. Box 388
Norwood, CO 81423
(303) 327-4261

Ouray Ranger District
2505 S. Townsend
Montrose, CO 81401
(303) 249-3711

Telluride Chamber of Commerce
P.O. Box 653
Telluride, CO 81435
(303) 728-3041

Further Reading

Historical Information

Aldrich, John K. *Ghost of...* series (booklets for Clear Creek, Gilpin, Park, Summit, Lake, Teller, Chaffee, Pitkin, and San Juan county ghost towns). Lakewood, Colorado: Centennial Graphics, 1986–1989.

Bancroft, Caroline. *Unique Ghost Towns and Mountain Spots.* Boulder, Colorado: Johnson Publishing Company, 1967.

Brown, Robert L. *Ghost Towns of the Colorado Rockies.* Caldwell, Idaho: Caxton Printers, 1968.

Dallas, Sandra. *Colorado Ghost Towns and Mining Camps.* Norman, Oklahoma: University of Oklahoma Press, 1985.

Digerness, David S. *The Mineral Belt: Volumes I, II, & III.* Silverton, Colorado: Sundance Publications, Ltd., 1977, 1978, 1982.

Eberhart, Perry. *Guide to the Colorado Ghost Towns and Mining Camps.* Chicago, Illinois: Sage Books, 1969.

Wolle, Muriel S. *Stampede to Timberline: The Ghost Towns and Mining Camps of Colorado.* Chicago, Illinois: Sage Books, 1974.

General Information on Mountain Biking

Bicycling Magazine. *Bicycling Magazine's Mountain Biking Skills*. Emmaus, Pennsylvania: Rodale Press, 1990.

Olsen, John. *Adventure Sports: Mountain Biking*. Harrisburg, Pennsylvania: Stackpole Books, 1990.

Strassman, Mike. *The Basic Essentials of Mountain Biking*. Merrillville, Indiana: ICS Books, Inc., 1989.

Van der Plas, Rob. *The Mountain Bike Book*. San Francisco, California: Bicycle Books, Inc., 1990.

Additional Mountain Bike Guides for Colorado

Anderson, James. *Mountain Biker's Guide to Crested Butte*. Crested Butte, Colorado: self-published, 1988.

Belmont, Barbara, and Compton, Richard. *Highwheeling: A Mountain Biker's Guide to Aspen and Snowmass*. Aspen, Colorado: self-published, 1987.

Boody, Carol J. *A Mountain Bike Guide for Cañon City, Colorado*. Cañon City, Colorado: self-published, 1989.

Bureau of Land Management and U.S. Forest Service. *Bicycle Routes on Public Lands of Southwest Colorado*. Durango, Colorado: no publisher, 1990.

Coello, Dennis. *Mountain Bike Rides of the West: Twenty Classic Tours*. Flagstaff, Arizona: Northland Publishing Company, 1989.

Harris, Bill. *Bicycling the Uncompahgre Plateau*. Ouray, Colorado: Wayfinder Press, 1988.

Moore, Rika N. *Mountain Biking in the Pikes Peak Area: Where to Ride Guide*. Colorado Springs, Colorado: self-published, 1989.

Nelson, David. *Ride Guide: Fifty Colorado Bike Routes from the Weekly Column*. Denver, Colorado: Denver Publishing Company, 1990.

Rossetter, Laura. *The Mountain Bike Guide to Summit County, Colorado*. Silverthorne, Colorado: Sage Creek Press, 1989.

Stoehr, William L. *Bicycling the Backcountry*. Boulder, Colorado: Pruett Publishing Company, 1987.

Stoehr, William L. *Mountain Bike Rides in the Colorado Front Range*. Boulder, Colorado: Pruett Publishing Company, 1988.